Table of Contents

How to Guidebook to the Internet Jungle Avoiding the scams and Traps

By: R. D. Krause

Any resemblance to actual persons, living or dead, events, or locales in this work are entirely coincidental.

Dedication

This work is dedicated to my dear friend and brother, Gerald "Ted" Connally. Who has sagely reminded me on many occasions to write what I know. Thank you my friend I hope you will continue to give me such valuable advice for many years to come.

Foreword

For the past thirty plus years I have been involved with the building and programming and repairing of that wonderful piece of equipment known as the Computer.

After retiring from government service back in 2008, I returned to school and acquired my degree in Network Engineering & Administration along with several professional certifications. I have concentrated on computer security and protection with my own consulting business which pertains mainly to and concentrates on that aspect of the field.

During that time I have sadly found that many very nice people find themselves victim to the attacks of the many criminals that populate the World Wide Web and Internet. Most of which were simply trying to find a way to supplement their income by operating an on-line at home business.

It was then that I decided that a guide book was needed to attempt to protect these gentle folk. By, teaching them how to recognize the "Red Flags" and pitfalls of this type of this type of endeavor.

Hopefully this book will save them from falling victim to these nefarious on- line scams, and cons, keeping them from having the pain of losing their hard earned cash on an endeavor that is designed to fail.

Chapter 1

A quick Introduction

Everyday hundreds, thousands, maybe hundreds of thousands of people decide to investigate the idea of working from home or starting their very own home-based business. They have heard of others that have done so who have been very successful...maybe even wildly successful at it.

Some of these people are very computer savvy individuals. They may even have the ability to build their own web pages. They certainly know the ins and outs of operating a computer. Others aren't all that computer savvy but they think they have a great idea for an Internet business and are sure that they can find a way to follow their dream.

The Internet really is the great equalizer. The level of formal education that a budding Internet entrepreneur has doesn't seem to have much bearing on the degree of success that they can achieve on the Internet or how much of a failure they can become. There are those who have reached dizzying heights of success who never finished high school and those who have hit rock bottom who have multiple college degrees.

The commonalities of those who succeed in either working from home or running a home-based business are:

> › They are all self-starters.
>
> › They have a positive attitude.
>
> › They are willing to learn.
>
> › They develop the necessary survival skills....it really is a jungle out there.

If you are considering starting, or have already started working from home or a home-based business, you are obviously a self-starter.

You wouldn't have even considered such a venture if you didn't have a positive attitude.

You are apparently willing to learn, you are reading this book.

The world of Internet business is the electronic equivalent of a jungle. In words made famous in "The Wizard of Oz", "There are lions and tigers and bears, oh my!" Survival and success aren't based on education. They are both based upon the mastering of survival skills.

Chapter 2

There are Lions

Funny! When you log onto the Internet, there is nothing that indicates that you have just entered an untamed jungle. You don't hear any roaring lions or other ominous sounds and you don't see any wild animals that are planning to have you as the main course for dinner but they are out there. They are just in disguise.

There is no particular order that you will meet these dangerous characters but some of the first ones that you are likely to meet are those that I like to think of as the 'welcoming committee'.

Selling what's Free

The object of this welcoming committee is to sell you what can be had for free all over the Internet if you know where to look.

Anti-Virus Protection

The first thing that you will be told that you must buy is anti-virus software. Now, there are some very good anti-virus programs out there that are being sold. But if your financial ability is somewhat limited, you really do not have to buy expensive anti-virus programs.

Yes, you must have an anti-virus program on your computer. There isn't any doubt about that one. The Internet is full of creeps that get their jollies by infecting computers with viruses, worms and Trojans. You don't want that to happen to you or your computer.

There are those that spend their every waking hour just dreaming up new and insidious ways of making problems for the rest of us. Luckily, there are just as many good folks out there that spend their time figuring out how to keep them from doing it to us.

Two of the best known anti-virus programs out there are Norton and McAfee and both of them are very good programs. Both of them are also rather expensive. McAfee is more expensive than Norton but neither one of them are really cheap and they are certainly not free.

However, there is also a very good one that is absolutely free. That one is AVAST I have personally use it for many years now and have ever yet had a problem with it. The definitions are updated on a daily basis and it has always worked to keep my systems free and clean of problems. AVAST has many anti-virus and other security programs available but they also have a free version which is the one that I use the most. This free version works very well and provides ample protection. You can find this free program at https://www.avast.com.

Firewalls

Most computers today come with built-in firewalls. Windows added that feature to XP. It is already on your computer when you bring it home.

Just because you already have a firewall that is sufficient to protect your computer, doesn't mean that there won't be members of the welcome-to-the-jungle committee who won't be trying to sell you one.

You will be told that the one that is on your computer has failed to protect you. You will see these little pop-ups telling you that you need to have your computer scanned.

The scan is, of course, free. The purpose of the scan is to sell you something that you don't need....usually a firewall, but there are other programs as well.

You already have a firewall and multiple firewalls do not add protection. They actually interfere with each other. You are better off to stick with the firewall that came built into your computer.

Instructional 'Courses'

There are many very good instructional courses available on the Internet. There are even more instructional courses on the Internet that are totally bogus. They only offer you information that is readily available for free and charge you large sums to provide it to you.

One of the very worst ones that I have seen promises to teach you 'data entry'. This course has absolutely nothing to do with data entry or data entry work. It 'teaches' you to sign up for affiliate programs and place ads in Google Ad Words for those products.

Affiliate marketing can be a very lucrative Internet business. It isn't learned easily but it is a real Internet business. This program tries to disguise affiliate marketing as data entry solely for the purpose of fooling young stay-at-home-moms, retired people, and others into spending fifty hard-earned bucks on a program that isn't going to be of any value to them at all if they are looking for a work-at-home job and aren't prepared or able to put in the hundred plus hours each week that are required to launch a successful affiliate marketing business.

Remember this. Anybody with dollar signs in their eyes, a computer and an Internet connection can advertise instructional programs. Some of these 'helpful' folks simply gather information that is readily available on the Internet, package it, write some slick advertising and then sell it to unsuspecting, hard working newbies who just haven't learned the ropes yet.

Before you ever sign up for a 'course' and pay money for it, do some research about the subject being 'taught' first and then ask yourself these questions:

Question #1: Can I find this information for myself?

Question #2: Is this information that I really need?

Question #3: Can this information really help me?

Question #4: Is the information being offered what it appears to be?

Question #5: Is there a guarantee?

Question #6: Will I be required to spend additional money to implement the information?

Question #7: How stiff will the competition be?

Question #8: Does the 'course' assume that I have more computer skills than I actually possess?

Question #9: Is the person teaching the course really knowledgeable or well-known?

Question #10: Does the advertisements sound too good to be true?

Disguised Pyramid Schemes

Pyramid schemes have been around since about the time the actual pyramids were built. You'd think that in the intervening few thousand years people would be able to easily recognize a pyramid scheme when they came face to face with one. The people who dream these things up, however, are pretty slick characters. A pyramid scheme never, ever, comes labeled as a pyramid scheme.

It is really easy to get sucked into one of these schemes. You need to understand how they work and be able to spot them for what they are. There are a few 'buzz' words that can tip you off:

1. Recruit: "to engage in finding and attracting employees, new members, students, athletes, etc." That's one of the definitions of the word according to the dictionary. The use of the word, 'recruit' (or

any variation) should be a major tip off that the program that is being promoted to you is most likely a pyramid scheme. Some of these schemes can be easily spotted while others are a little harder to identify. Just beware when you see the word, 'recruit'. There was a scheme that went around awhile back that was sent by unsolicited email that offered an 'exclusive opportunity' to earn a boat load of money by recruiting people to sell a device that would provide access to the Internet by television. No, I'm not kidding. This happened and people fell for it.

2. 'Buy the secret and sell....' This is a typical pyramid scheme that you will often see. This is another 'offer' that arrives in your inbox that you have not solicited. You are offered an 'exclusive' opportunity to buy a secret that will allow you to make a hundred thousand dollars a month (no work required) and then you can sell this secret to others for a substantial profit and they will make money for you. These gullible folks will just fill your bank account with beautiful green-backs. Wait! You are the gullible folk they are targeting.

You can believe me when I tell you that there really aren't a lot of people out there in this world that are eagerly awaiting the opportunity to send you money.

You can also believe that there is no legitimate Internet business that is going to immediately make you hundreds of thousands of dollars a month. You might someday make that kind of money but if you do, it will be after you have put in an incredible amount of time and effort and not because you bought a 'secret'...there isn't one.

3. 'Let others do the work': This little phrase has pyramid scheme written all over it. The 'pitch' is usually for a non-existent product. You will be sent information buy bulk mail that gives you instructions for getting other's to promote this 'product' and all you will have to do is count your millions. Right! Don't fall for that one.

Disguised MLM

If you are really new to the world of internet business or work-at-home job opportunities, you may not know what MLM means. It means **M**ulti-**L**evel-**M**arketing. MLM is similar to a pyramid scheme but it isn't exactly the same.

True pyramid schemes don't involve the selling of an actual product but MLM is all about selling an actual product.

According to Wikipedia, "Multilevel Marketing is selling products by using independent distributors and allowing these distributors to build and manage their own sales force by recruiting, motivating, supplying, and training others to sell products. The distributors' compensation includes their own sales and a percentage of the sales of their sales group (down line).

"So," you say, "that just sounds like a good idea for making money." Well, it is a good way for making money. The problem is that it is illegal.

Do you see that tip-off word, 'recruiting'? The other tip-off that this is a MLM scheme is the phrase, 'percentage of sales'.

There is nothing illegal about setting up and affiliate program and PAYING a percentage of sales to those who sell your products or services to others. There is nothing illegal about COLLECTING the percentages that are offered by the producers of the products or services. That is simply good business and a more than just common practice in the Internet business world.

The problem arises when you start COLLECTING percentages of sales from people whom you have recruited to sell the product. Then another level is added and it becomes multi-level marketing. Even one additional level is illegal but there are MLM schemes that will have many, MANY layers.

The main Internet banking and money exchange on the Internet is Paypal. Paypal employs full-time personnel to search for and identify MLM schemes. When these schemes are uncovered, the account (and all attached accounts and credit cards) are frozen.

Yes, it is true that sometimes Paypal does misidentify a perfectly legitimate business as a MLM scheme but it doesn't happen very often and the problem can usually be resolved in just two or three business days. This very thing happened to a friend of mine not long ago. It was resolved but not without him being able to prove that his business was not a MLM scheme.

This does point out the fact, however, that there are those who are looking for illegal MLM schemes. You may think that you are very anonymous on the Internet but when you do business on the Internet you are not longer anonymous.

Beware of Lions

There are a lot of big hungry lions in the Internet jungle. They are looking for easy marks...they love newbies best of all.

Chapter 3
There are Tigers

There are so many ways that newbies can 'be had' on the Internet. It is just sad that so many of those that are eaten up by the tigers that roam through the Internet jungle are only trying to find a way to be able to make some money using their personal computers and their Internet connections. They aren't even hoping to become rich or famous. They don't expect making money to be easy or fast. They simply want a job that will allow them to stay at home with their young children, help to put a loved child through collage or add to their retirement income. They are honest, hard-working decent people....that make the tigers out there start thinking about lunch.

Work-from-home

If you are considering trying to find a work at home job, you need to know that you will be working more hours for less money than you made at your job that was located in the brick and mortar world. On the other hand, you will not have all of the related expenses of a brick and mortar job either.

> You will not have the expense of traveling to and from work.

> You will not have the expense of suitable clothing for work.

> You will not have the expense of day-care.

> You will not have the expense of lunch out everyday.

Good things...all of them! But there is a downside to working from home, as well.

> You will be considered to be self-employed by the powers that be.

> You will have to pay all of your FICA tax. (Your employer now pays half.)

> You will have to convince your family and friends that you really do have a job. Trust me this can be a real problem, like writing books, yes my loves it really is work!

› You had better be aware of the tigers and other critters that want to have you for lunch...as the entree.

There are schemes and scams out there that are directed at those who want to be work-at-home moms, those who are looking for an additional income source and those who are retirees looking for part-time work to supplement their incomes. Some of these scams are:

Stuffing envelopes:

"Make extra money by stuffing envelopes from home!" This tiger is a bit long in the tooth. It's been around for years. Advertisements for 'at-home-envelope stuffers can be found in newspapers at your local library that date back several decades....and yet people will still fall for it.

The reason that people will fall for this ploy is that they get all of that unsolicited mail at their own homes and they think that somebody had to have put that paper into those envelopes that are addressed to them.

Nope! Sorry.... but no living person actually put that paper into those envelopes. It was put there by a machine and it was addressed by a computer. It was mailed in bulk.

There is always, of course, a 'small fee' to get started in the envelope stuffing business. In return for this, 'small fee' you will most likely get instructions for placing ads just like the one you fell for to get others to bite.

It is tiger...it is a con...and the only way that you will ever get your money back is to fool others into thinking they can make money by stuffing envelopes.

Fact: There is no envelope stuffing jobs to be had!

Craft or assembly jobs:

This tiger is very attractive. It appeals to those who are talented at crafts or handy with hand tools. These folks see an advertisement that promises them that they can make a ton of money by just doing what they already know how to do and are very good at and it is just almost irresistible. This looks like the opportunity that they have been looking for!

Whoa there my lovelies! Put that sewing machine or those hand tools away and let's think this over. There are some things that you don't know. There isn't any reason for you to know these things but you better learn them.....fast.

The headline of this advertisement is in big bold print and there are usually multiple exclamation points, as well. The headline promises that you will be sent the material and then be paid for the finished products when you send them in to the employer.

Don't skip the print that isn't quite as big as that headline. That's where the 'catch' is.....or, maybe I should say, catches. There's more than one way for this tiger to get you.

Usually the first thing is that you will be required to 'invest' in some special equipment or supplies that aren't going to be included in the 'free materials' that were promised in the larger print. This equipment or supplies can run anywhere from a few dollars to several hundred dollars. **This is what the advertisers are selling!** You will see that there is a no return policy for the equipment or supplies that you must purchase....there never are.

If you get out your magnifying glass and read the itty-bitty print at the very bottom that is well below the scroll line, you will see a statement that says something like, "All work must meet quality standards." It will look something like this: "All work must meet quality standards." That's where this tiger is really going to get you and get you good.

No work will ever meet quality standards. It isn't possible. You will buy the equipment or supplies. You will work to create the products as directed. You will never see one thin dime in payment for the finished products that you send.

It gets worse. You have no legal recourse. You agreed to buy the equipment or supplies and were told that there was a 'no return' policy. You agreed to produce products that met 'quality control standards' that were not specified. You've been had!

The fact is that there really is a huge market for hand-crafted products out there. The market is huge...maybe almost unlimited. If you have a talent for making hand-crafted products and if you have the ability to market them, you can make some money doing it.

You will not, however, ever make any money just using your talents to assemble hand-crafted products at home for these tigers that are not even selling them. They are selling the equipment and supplies....that is ALL they are selling...and they want to sell them to you.

Fact: You can make money selling hand crafted items but not by assembling these items for others.

Medical Billing:

This very large headline will read something like, "Job explosion in the Health Care Industry!!!!!!!" There are always a lot of exclamation points. You will see these advertisements in newspapers, magazines and, of course, on the Internet.

You will be told that the entire reason that medical costs are so high is because the medical profession needs your personal assistance and that just by taking a job, for which you will be very well paid, you can single-handedly lower the cost of health care for the whole world. Wow!

You need a job...and they need you! Sounds like a partnership that would work out well for everybody.

These advertisements try to sell you on the idea that it's the overwhelming amount of required paperwork that is the root cause of the inflation of health care costs....for all of us.

These advertisements claim that all that is needed to fix this problem in the implementation of electronic claim processing....which is a new and innovative technology that has recently become available.

Horse feathers! Electronic billing is done by a few well established companies. Doctors subscribe to these services and have been doing so for more than a few years. Medical billing isn't done by hand and hasn't been since the late 1980's.

If you answer one of the advertisements, what you will get in return for the hard-earned dollars that you send in is a brochure, an application, some discs, a contract, some disclosure statements (in tiny print), and possibly some testimonial letters from people who will swear that this has changed their lives and made the wealthy beyond their wildest dreams. HA!

What you will have are some basic instructions for setting up your own medical billing business. What you will not have is a medical building job. You will be required to get your own clients. They will not be supplied. As I said before, there are a few (and only a few) well established companies that have been doing this billing for doctors for many years. They are your competition...and very stiff competition.

You will be promised that you can earn a ton of bucks by only working part time and at your own pace. Now stop just a minute and think about that. Part time AND a ton of money? Does that really sound reasonable to you? It isn't a reasonable expectation. You aren't likely to make a ton of money working at a full time job of any kind and you certainly won't be making very much, if anything, by working part time. Real world business doesn't work like that and neither does Internet based businesses.

Oh, and you will also be required to make a personal investment of between one and TEN thousand dollars in order to get in on the golden opportunity.

Fact: Medical billing is well covered by the few companies who have been doing it for decades. You aren't the answer to the soaring cost of health care.

Data Entry:

No doubt you can picture yourself just putting numbers in columns for a few hours a day from the comfort of your own home and making enough money by doing it to make up your financial short fall, right? No...sorry....that isn't really very likely to happen.

I'm not telling you that there are NO data entry jobs available. I am only telling you that you aren't likely to get one of them by answering one of those slick ads that promise you a data entry job if you will but sign up for their course.

The problem with these so-called data entry courses, is that they rarely have anything to do with data entry jobs. Most of them are more on the order of teaching you (more or less) how to set up and run your own affiliate program.

There isn't anything wrong with affiliate programs but they aren't data entry jobs. They are businesses in which you will do some data entry work....like on tax forms when you file your self-employment tax returns. There can also be data entry work in the operation of an affiliate marketing business. You will need to enter data in order to maintain orderliness in your business.

If you let this tiger get you, after you pay you money you will get a course that will either be delivered electronically via the computer, on CD's or DVD's. This course will teach how to find affiliate programs that you can sign up for (information that is readily available for free on the Internet). Then you will be instructed how to set up advertisements in Google Ad Words (this information is also readily available on the Internet). What you will not be told is that affiliate marketing is an extremely competitive business. It isn't a data entry job. You will be told that these ads that you have to se up in Google Ad words will only cost you one penny each. Now there is a big fat, out-and-out, rotten lie.

You might set up ads that will only cost you one penny each time someone clicks on them....that much is true. Your ads will be listed on about page 15 in search results and you aren't very likely to have them clicked on. But if, by some stroke of luck, they are clicked on, they cost well more than one penny per click.

Fact: Nearly all Data entry courses are a scam. They will not secure a data entry job for you. No matter what they say or promise!

Writers Wanted:

Here's is yet another tiger that is out to make you the main course for his dinner. It is absolutely true that the Internet gobbles up words at an alarming rate and that there is always a demand for those who can write articles, ebooks and reports about a variety of subjects.

Writing for the Internet is an art. Just because you can string sentences together that are grammatically correct and make sense doesn't mean that you can write for Internet marketers.

The advertisements that you see that say, 'Writers Wanted' don't really want writers. What they want are the people who want to be writers. There will always be a course you are required to pay for or a list that you are required to buy. That's what these advertisements are selling....courses or lists....they are NOT selling writing jobs.

Trust me, I know of what I speak, for I myself have been the victim of this one in my early days of writing!

Fact: You will not get a job writing by taking a course or buying a list.

Check List

There really are work-at-home jobs out there. The problem is finding the ones that are legitimate job offers. So many, are nothing more than Internet jungle tigers waiting to take advantage of you. Here is a check list that will help you to separate the fact from the fiction:

1. What is the 'cost' of getting the job that is advertised? Find out what, if any, equipment or supplies are required. Legitimate work-at-home jobs do not

require that you spend money. They pay YOU money.

1. Tell me what the tasks are that I must perform in order to get paid. This is a legitimate question to ask. Every job on earth comes with a job description of some kind. If the company or individual that you are talking to can describe the job is a few sentences, keep looking.
2. Is this a salaried position or will I be paid on a commission or hourly basis? Here's another one question that any potential employee shouldn't hesitate to ask. Pay is always based upon something. It is either paid as a salary that has nothing whatsoever to do with hours worked or it is based upon an hourly pay scale for which you will be required to sign in and sign out or it is based upon a commission of percentage of sales that you must make.

1. Who pays me and when? That's an easy question. Every single legitimate company or individual employer has regular and specified pay periods. You might be paid once a week, once a month or twice a month. Any of those pay period options are perfectly legitimate.

1. Where are you located? This is a question that only someone who is working from home would have to ask. If you were working in the brick and mortar

world, you would be well aware of the place where you were expected to report to work. The Internet presents another little problem. We are all connected electronically rather that physically. You might be working for someone who is located in Malaysia. You need to be told where the person or business is physically located.

1. How will I receive instructions? Here again, this is a problem that only comes up when the job is being done on the computer. You may receive instructions by email or by way of an instant messaging service.

1. Who will I receive instructions from? This is a question that might need to be answered for real world businesses as well as for online ones. Many times there will be more than one partner in an online business. You need to know who it is that will supply you with instructions and directions. You don't want to have to decide who to take direction from.

What Can You Do if the Tiger Gets You?

You are not likely to ever recover any money that you have paid to the work-at-home scam artists have taken you for. Of course, it never hurts to try. Who knows? You might get lucky and at the very least you might prevent another person from getting taken in.

You might even make it hard enough on a work-at-home scam artist to make him think he has a tiger by the tail.

1. The Federal Trade Commission is the government entity charged with the protection of consumers. Call them at 1-877-FTC-HELP (1-877-382-4357). That is the place to report fraudulent business practices.

1. If you live in a metropolitan area, there is most likely a consumer protection office in your area. You can call them or write them.

1. Report the offending business to the Better Business Bureau. This sometimes seems to be an exercise in futility but it does have a direct impact on businesses.

1. If any part of the correspondence came to you through the USPS, you can contact your local postmaster to report it. Mail fraud is a federal crime.

1. You can contact the Attorney General of the state in which the company or individual is based. They may well have violated some state laws in the process of scamming you.

Frankly, it just makes my blood boil when I see these slick advertisements that are aimed directly at those that are least able to absorb the cost of being scammed.

There may be very little that you can actually do to undo the damage that they have caused you, but by putting forth some time and effort you may prevent them from doing the same thing to others.

Chapter 4

There are Bears

The bears that live and unfortunately thrive in the Internet jungle come in several varieties. Out in the real world you only find a few kinds but on the Internet there are many more.

Being ambitious is not a crime. It is an admirable quality and one that you should be proud of. Wanting to do better is what has made this country great. It's the corner stone of every fortune that has ever been built.

Wanting to better yourself and being willing to roll up your sleeves and do the work necessary to achieve a better life for yourself and your family is also the cornerstone of success in the world of Internet business.

Many people want a job and there is nothing wrong with wanting a job but others want to be their own boss. They want to be the one who gives orders and not the one who takes orders. They want to make the decisions and not just carry out decisions that have been made by others. They want to be captains of their own ships and masters of their own destinies....there is nothing wrong with that either. It is to be admired.

Ambition is good but it can also be dangerous. An eagerness to succeed can cause you to forget that you are living in a jungle that is fraught with danger on every side.

There are big ugly bears out there just waiting for you to forget for one minute that they are out to get you. They are waiting for you to get careless. They are waiting for you to let ambition cloud your judgment.

For every one ambitious, hard-working, honest Internet entrepreneur out there, there are at least a thousand under-handed, crooked bears waiting to take advantage of them.

Successful internet businesses can be created. They HAVE been created. You can create one yourself if you are willing to put in the time, effort, energy and, yes, money that is required. A successful Internet business will not be created over night and anybody who promises you that it is an easy and painless process is lying to you.

Don't underestimate the bears. They are very, very good at what they do. They have fooled some of the best of them.

MLM schemes:

We have briefly discussed Multi-Level Marketing schemes before but there is a lot more that you need to know so that you won't get suckered into one of these schemes and become a bear yourself.

MLM schemes are illegal and if even if you get suckered into becoming a part of one, you are just as guilty as the person you involved you. Ignorance of the law is not an acceptable excuse.

These 'plans' for success on the Internet come packaged and presented in ways that make it difficult to identify them as MLM schemes. They do, however, all have some things in common. The most obvious and the easiest to spot sign is that you are offered a commission for sales of products or services that are made by others....this is above and beyond any commission payments for sales that you make yourself. That's the thing that makes these plans MLM. You will be paying part of your commission to the person who recruited you and you will be receiving commission payments from people whom you recruit, as will, the person who recruited you and the person who recruited them.

The only limit to the number of levels that can be achieved in a MLM scheme is the point at which it collapses in on itself. Did I mention that the pyramid is an upside down one? The point is at the bottom...not at the top. There is always a point at which the scheme will collapse. When it gets heavy enough at the top, it will come tumbling down. You do not want to be anywhere near the point of collapse. As a matter of fact, you don't want to be anywhere near the pyramid at all.

Do you recall 'chain letters'? Chain letters are started by a person of a group of people and they prey on the greed of others. The first person starts a letter and collects $1000 from each of the next nine people. Each of those nine people recruit (there's that word again) others to send them a $1000 each...and on and on the pyramid builds until it gets top heave and collapses. That is precisely what happens in an MLM scheme except that there is always a product involved in an MLM scheme and there isn't ever a product involved in a pyramid scheme.

So how do you know for sure what is really an MLM scheme? Here's a check list that will help you to avoid this bear:

1. Are you required to recruit others in order to make money?. If the answer to that question is 'yes', it would be a pretty good bet that it is in fact an MLM scheme.

1. Do I have to buy any inventory? Remember....there is ALWAYS a product involved in an MLM scheme. If you are required to purchase inventory, you may well be looking at an MLM scheme.

1. If you see the words, 'downline commissions' anywhere....especially in the fine print...this is definitely an MLM scheme. 'Downline Commissions' means a percentage of a commission that someone else has been paid.

1. Others have made millions! Oh, did you believe those glowing testimonials that you read? Anybody can write a testimonial. I could write one for myself or my business and sign anybody's name to it and so could you. There is never a way in an MLM scheme to check out the 'testimonials'. It simply isn't possible. Even if you are given addresses and phone numbers or email addresses, you have no way to be certain that these testimonials are fact and not just a lot of marketing hype.

Fact: MLM schemes are illegal. Be certain that you are not drawn into one because then you are guilty of fraud.

E-mail processing:

This is a bear that is very much like the enveloping stuffing one that preys on those seeking a work-at-home job but it is hungry for the person who wants an Internet business of their own rather than just a job. Rather than say, 'envelope stuffing' it says, 'email processing'.

This bear only wants you to take fifty bucks away from you. He says that for that very low price, you can start your very own business and work at your leisure from the comfort of your own home. You can be your own boss. You can just work when you want to.

Now wait just a minute here! Back up that mail truck and let's take a look at what is really inside this offer.

First of all, who do you think needs email 'processed' and what is processing? I've seen advertisements that claim you can make up to $25 dollars just for processing a single email.

You have an email account yourself. Go look at it and see which of your emails would need to be processed. I can tell you....none of them.....and nobody else has email that needs to be processed either.

This isn't a business opportunity. It's a bear. If you send in your $50, what you will get in return is a set of poorly written instructions telling you how to place the same ad that you fell for and get other people to send you $50 each.

That doesn't sound like a legitimate Internet business, does it? It isn't one. The only thing that you will gain from falling for this will be a wallet that is $50 lighter.

You want to be the proud owner of a successful and legitimate internet business. You don't want to become a scam artist or a bear yourself.

E-Mail Marketing Business:

While it is certainly true that many people do make very nice incomes sending out marketing emails that advertise products, it just is not as simple as the ads telling you that you can send emails and make money make it sound. You can become an email marketer but you must build your own list of people to market to.

What these advertisements are selling is a list of names and email addresses. Understand that anytime you see an advertisement telling you that you can make boat loads of money, there will ALWAYS be a product that is being sold. Selling this product is the way that the people who placed these ads plan on making THEIR boat load of money...not YOURS.

Back in 2003 the United States Congress passed the **CAN-SPAM Act**. It became the law of the land in January 2004. **CAN-SPAM** is an acronym for **Controlling the Assault of Non-Solicited Pornography and Marketing.**

The **CAN-SPAM Act** states that sending unsolicited bulk email is a crime. The Act is enforced be the Federal Trade Commission and they really are not kidding. There are fines and penalties for violations of the Act that go up to $11,000 per incident that are handed down by the Department of Justice.

Legitimate internet marketers, those who sell their own products and services, as well as, those who sell products and services of others (Affiliate Marketers), all have what are known as 'opt-in' lists. These are lists of people who have agreed to allow these legitimate merchants to send them email. The **CAN-SPAM Act** is not being violated if you have permission to send bulk email.

When you buy a list of names and email addresses, you do not have permission to send bulk email to the names on that list. I know....I know....the sellers of these lists will tell you that they have the right to give you permission to send email. **They DO NOT have that right.** The one and only person who can give you permission to send bulk email to their inboxes is the person who owns that email address...the recipient. Third parties cannot give you that permission.

There are many legitimate list building techniques. None of these techniques are easy and they are certainly not fast. You can write and market ebooks and articles, you can post to blogs and forums, you can do a lot of legal things to build your own opt-in list but you cannot BUY a legal opt-in list no matter what those ads tell you.

If this bear get you, it can end up costing you millions of dollars. There really aren't any shortcuts to having a successful online business.

Fact: Sending unsolicited bulk email is a crime according to the CAN-SPAM Act of 2003. The penalties are stiff.

1-900 Business Opportunities:

This bear has claws and teeth. You will see an advertisement that says something like, "Call 1-900-555-5555 to discover your pot of gold!!!!!"

It is sad but it is true that it is perfectly legal to advertise a 900 number. Unlike 800 numbers or 866 numbers, the 900 number call is NOT free. Not only is it not 'free' the cost per minute is set by the owner of the number and can be exorbitant.

The advertisements are slick and very convincing. When you call one of these 900 numbers, your telephone company will be charging you by the minute. Fees per minute can be a few dollars or quite a few dollars. You will be kept on the phone for as long as possible. You will be given information on how to set up your own 900 number (that's the secret that you are paying for) and how to place advertisements to get others to call your 900 number.

When you get your next telephone bill, you may go into cardiac arrest because it is likely to be well over $1000. You will have no recourse. You will either pay the bill or your telephone company will disconnect your service.

The person who placed the advertisement gets most of the money that you will pay your telephone company.

FACT: Never call a 1-900 number! You do not know how much you will be charged per minute for the call and the 'secret' that you will be given access to is just how to pull the same dirty trick on others.

Instant Riches Can Be Yours!

This bear is used by many different crooks and scam artists. The body of the advertisement changes with the tides or the seasons but the message remains the same.

The message is that you can become unbelievably wealthy overnight if you just know how. The bears that place these advertisements are preying upon your ambition. Your ambition is a good thing but you must remember that is also bear bait.

Do you remember when the 'Dot-Com Bubble' burst in 2000? For several years prior to the burst of the bubble, many bright-eyed-bushy-tailed young entrepreneurs made millions overnight. They lost those millions overnight, as well.

Here is the bottom line of all Internet business opportunities: You can be a successful online business entrepreneur.....IF and ONLY IF....you are willing to put in the time, effort, energy, and money to become successful. That success is not going to come overnight. You might appear to be an overnight success to your friends and families but YOU will know better.

Fact: Overnight fortunes are never made overnight. They are the product of a lot of hard work and devotion to a dream. Don't believe the hype.

Become a Blogging Millionaire:

When this bear came out of the woods, I was just sure that nobody would buy into the scheme. I was wrong. A lot of people have fallen for this.

The 'pitch' is that all you have to do is just set up a blog (you can do this for free) and then sell high priced advertising space to big multimillion dollar companies. You are told that these huge companies have stacks of cash lying around just waiting for you to claim it.

Yes, blogging is big on the Internet at the moment but you won't be making millions by starting your own blog. Blogging is a tool that is used by many very successful Internet marketers but it is not a business unto itself.

There may well be a few blogs that are owned and operated by people who are famous or infamous that make money selling advertising space. Yours is not going to be one of them.

You always must ask the question: "What is the promoter getting out of this offer?" You can bet your boots that they aren't doing all this advertising for YOUR benefit and to help

YOU get rich. They are selling something that will make money for THEM.

In this case, the blogging website is free but the information that, according to them, you MUST have comes at a price. For just a few hundred bucks they can tell you how to turn your blog into a "money-making machine".

Do you have any idea how many blog sites there are on the Internet? Me either but I can tell you that there are a lot more than a few. Huge multimillion dollar International corporations are not going to pay you for advertising space on your little blog website.

Fact: You aren't going to make millions selling advertising space on your blog site.

There are many legitimate ways to start and succeed at running an online business. You are to be greatly admired for wanting to do better for yourself and for your family.

You do, however, need to understand that succeeding in the world of Internet commerce isn't going to happen overnight. It isn't even going to happen over many nights. Succeeding at anything takes a lot of your time, effort and energy and succeeding at Internet commerce isn't an exception to that rule.

There are a lot of bears out there in the Internet jungle that will try to convince you that there are shortcuts that can make you successful and wealthy overnight. The bears are lying!

Chapter 5
Oh, My!

That's what Dorothy said in the 'Wizard of Oz'.....'There are lions and tigers and bears! Oh, my!" Out there on the World Wide Web, there really are lions and tigers and bears, as well as, other critters that can eat you alive, make your life miserable, or rob you of your dreams and ambitions.

The dangerous jungles creatures are also very smart jungle creatures. They all have opposable thumbs and are capable of setting traps for you to fall into. The 'bait' they use to get you, the unsuspecting newbie' to fall into these insidious traps is 'help'.

They trick you into believing that what they are offering you is help when, in fact, what they are doing is tricking you into falling into their traps. Some bait that is used is:

You have been CHOSEN:

This little piece of bait usually arrives in your inbox. It is nothing that you solicited so it IS SPAM but it is very clever SPAM. The email will say something like, "You have been chosen to participate in a_______________!!

The blank can be filled in many ways. One of the ways that went around for awhile, and may still be making the rounds, is "You have been chosen to participate in a program that is marketing walk-up Internet access."

All you have to do, since you have been CHOSEN, is to buy this machine that will be installed in a 'high-traffic' area close to where you live. Then you can just go pick up your money whenever you find the time.

They imply that you can easily find the time to go pick up your money between flying by personal jet to play golf with Donald Trump and having dinner with the President. Snap!

You send in your several thousand dollars to purchase (or lease) this machine then you have absolutely no control over where the machine is places...IF it is placed. It can be put in a low traffic dimly it corner of a dive in the sleaziest part of town...it isn't up to you. Oh, My!

You are SO SMART!

Well, everybody likes to be thought of as intelligent, don't they? This is very good bait! It is designed to make you believe that FINALLY somebody realizes just how smart you really are.

Again, this bait usually arrives in your inbox and it is SPAM. The offer tells you that because you are such an intelligent person, you can become an Internet Consultant and earn millions just by advising others. Sometimes you will also see these kinds of advertisements on websites as well.

But, wait just a minute! Didn't you just get here? Aren't you still considered a newbie in the world of Internet commerce? What exactly do you know and what can kind of advise can you give? Ah.....but the critters that baited this trap will gladly tell you everything you need to know so that you can become a highly paid and sought after 'consultant'.....for a price. Oh, My!

You are SO HONEST!

Well, of course you are honest. You know that, you just didn't realize that others were aware of this fine quality.

This offer for a credit card or a guaranteed loan is made by unsolicited email sometimes but you can also see these advertisements in trade magazines and in newspapers.

They tell you that, even if you are young and aren't well established financially or even if you have had credit difficulties in the past, THEY know that you are an honest person and they are willing to help you because you are such an honest person. You will see the word, 'honest' repeated often in these advertisements.

You are told that you can get a home equity loan even if you don't have any equity in your home. You are told that you can get a credit card with a really high spending limit no matter what your credit history is.

These offers are most often Ponzi schemes (which we will discuss later) or they are an attempt to get your personal information for the purpose of identity theft.

Oh, My!

You DESERVE our help!

Somewhere inside all of us mere mortals there is a little place that tells us that we really ARE deserving of the better things in life. That is just a fact of human nature and one that can be used as bait by the Internet jungle critters to lure you into their traps.

Not always, but certainly most of the time, people do get what the deserve. If you work hard and long you will most likely succeed and if you don't, you most likely won't. But we aren't born DESERVING anything. We make our own luck and we build our own success. This is another bait that the Internet critters use to trick you. Don't take the bait.

Sometimes this bait is used to lure you into making risky investments. Many times the Internet jungle animals believe that because you are in business for yourself, you must have a ton of disposable income and they want to get their greedy little hands on some of it. So they place advertisements that tell you that you DESERVE to participate in the LIMITED offer. The offer is only limited by the number of people who actually take this bait.

A lot of these offers that are made because you are so deserving of them are pushing off-shore bank accounts or land in foreign countries. Many are MLM or Ponzi schemes.

Some of these offers are for free goods or services. After all, you DESERVE to get stuff for free. The offer will be a membership in a 'buying club'. Of course, there really are many legitimate buying clubs that really do offer great discounts on brand name merchandize. There offers will not, however, arrive in your inbox unsolicited. Oh, My!

You can be NUMBER ONE!

Okay, who doesn't want to be number one? There is a tiny little problem, however. There is only ONE number one spot and only one person or company can occupy that position. Promising to make you number one is very good bait.

When you see advertisements that guarantee you the NUMBER ONE spot in Google search results, stop just a minute and think about that promise. How many number one spots are there? There is ONE...so how can this company promise to make everybody number one and deliver on that promise? Answer: they can't deliver. They can, however, collect a lot of money for themselves.

If that amazing offer appeared in your inbox, you can bet your bottom dollar that it is part of a mass mailing that went out to hundreds of thousands of other people just like you. If you see an advertisement for such an offer, you don't think that it was placed just for you, do you? How many people do you think will see the same advertisement?

Here are the hard cold facts about rankings in Google search results (or rankings in any search engine results for that matter). The top Internet marketers, the guys and gals who really do make tons of money marketing on the Internet, struggle for YEARS to gain a Page Rank of 7 or better. Top page ranks in a search results is one of the hardest tasks in all Internet marketing.

There is NOBODY that can promise (and keep the promise) to make you number one in search engine results. There are ways to improve your PR in search engine results....all of which take time, effort and know-how.

Writing and marketing articles and ebooks, posting to blogs and forums, doing link exchanges, etc are all proven PR rank improvements techniques. There is no magic formula. Don't take this bait! Oh, My!

Success can be EASY for YOU!

Everybody looks for an easier way to do everything. Hey....why do you think the wheel and the lever were invented? We all want to do as little work as possible to achieve our goals. You aren't the only one. "Easy for You" is a bait that is wildly successful for that very reason.

These advertisements sometimes arrive as unsolicited mail in your inbox but they can also be found splashed all over the Internet and in newspapers and magazines. Easy riches! Wow!

They tell you that only fools work hard to make money. They say that making money is so easy that it is basically a 'no-brainer'. They shout that hard work is overrated and a totally unnecessary complication that YOU don't have to be burdened with. ALL you have to do, they say, is take their advice, which they will happily supply to you for a price.

There are those in this world who really do have a lot of money that they didn't work for. They were born rich or they hit the lottery or a long lost rich uncle died and left them millions. You have a better chance of being struck by lightening than you have of having millions without putting in the blood sweat and tears that are required to earn them. So...SNAP!

This bait is designed to take whatever money you do have out of your pocket and put it in the pockets of these jungle critters. THEY certainly don't intend to work for their money. Oh, My!

You can learn the SECRETS of Success!

Do you know what a secret is? It's a piece of information that isn't common knowledge. It is something that is whispered into listening ears. Ah....but we all want to know the 'secrets'. What great bait! Secrets!

You will be inundated with offers from those who will reveal their secrets of success to you. Almost every time that you opt-in to a list or sign up for a marketing course of any kind, you will be promised that you are going to learn some 'secrets'.

Now, some courses and seminars really do provide useful inside information to budding Internet entrepreneurs but the information is hardly a secret. It might be gems of knowledge gained through experience. It could be bits of wisdom or even some very good advice.

The trick to knowing which of the thousands of courses, seminars, tele-seminars or webinars that you can really benefit from, is knowing who the leaders of the authors of the courses or the leaders and speakers of events are. You need to know what their backgrounds are.

You can learn a lot from those who have blazed trails...but they won't be secrets. Really successful Internet marketers have a lot they can teach you and much wisdom they can share but everybody is NOT a successful Internet marketer who offers to reveal secrets to you.

One way to check out whom really successful Internet marketers are and who are just jungle beasts that want your money, is to plug names of authors or speakers into the search box of your favorite search engine. You can learn a lot about people if you just look around the Internet.

Don't believe everything you read. Check out the credentials of authors or speakers before you pay for the information they are offering. Don't take the bait! Oh, My!

You can learn to SELL Anything!

"Everyone lives by selling something." - Robert Louis Stevenson (1850-1894) Scottish novelist, poet.

How true! We all sell something. We sell our time or our knowledge or we sell a product or a service. Everybody is selling something. Some of us do it better than others.

There is, however, a catch to selling. You have to have something of value to sell before you will have any paying customers. Hype won't cut it.

There is no doubt that effective selling techniques exist. There is no doubt that some of these techniques can be taught. But....you can't actually learn to sell ANYTHING. You can sell something. You can sell merchandize or services that have value. But you can't sell just ANYTHING!

Many marketers, those of the brick and mortar world and those of the Internet marketing world, have found out that selling is only the first part of a process. The second part is that the customer who buys whatever is being sold has untold power. Today, if the customer isn't happy, they usually have a recourse. If you sell inferior products, you will get a lot of returns and you will have your credibility severely damaged.

Selling isn't all that hard if you have a good product or a good service that will satisfy the customers who purchase it. You have to keep it sold. You don't want returns.

Being a good salesman can be learned. Selling an honest product or service will keep it sold.

You really can't sell just ANYTHING! Oh, My!

Chapter 6

There are Sneaky Snakes

Yes, indeed! There are "lions and tigers and bears, oh my!" But the Internet jungle is also populated with sneaky snakes. These slimy creatures can sneak up on you and have you wrapped up, tied with a red bow and have your pocket picked before you know it.

The Ponzi scheme is one such sneaky snake ploy that isn't all that easy to identify. On the surface it appears to be a perfectly legitimate business enterprise.

You may be wondering how the Ponzi Scheme got its name. There was a person by the name of Ponzi....Charles Ponzi. He was born in Italy in 1882 and migrated to the United States as a very young man of a tender 21 years in 1903. He was a poor boy. He had only two dollars and fifty cents in his pocket when he landed on our shores. He was poor but he had big dreams and a whole boat load of ambition...not to mention a propensity for shady dealing. He pulled off one of the worse swindling schemes in history...so bad that the swindle bears his name...the Ponzi Scheme.

He stole some money, got caught, went to prison, met a man by the name of Charles Morse and learned that rich people can get away with almost anything. He decided to become rich.

He married a woman named Rose Gnecco in 1918. He suffered through several failed business ventures. One such failed adventure was a catalog similar to what we know today as the yellow pages. His business failed shortly after he launched this campaign but a few weeks later he received a letter from a company in Spain asking about the catalog. Included in the letter was a 'postal coupon'. Ponzi didn't know what it was so he asked. He found out that the postal coupon was way in which a company could send mail to a foreign company and include a postal coupon so that the person could reply at no cost to themselves.

I won't go into great detail here. If you want to read about the details of the scheme, click here[1]. What the deal amounted to was buying postal coupons in countries with low rates and cashing them in countries with high rates. It was a form of currency trading....which is illegal. He claimed that after expenses he was making a 400% profit and easily attracted investors into his scheme.

The scheme was a complicated but very effective one....albeit illegal. Ponzi, of course, got greedier and began convincing more investors to sink large sums into his company and using those funds to pay former investors.

"A fraudulent investment operation that involves paying returns to investors out of the money raised from subsequent investors, rather than from profits generated by any real

1. http://en.wikipedia.org/wiki/Ponzi

business. A Ponzi scheme offers high short-term returns in order to entice new investors, whose money is needed to fund payouts to earlier investors, and to lure its victims into ever-bigger risks" is the way in which Wikapedia defines a Ponzi scheme.

Charles Ponzi died in 1949 but his name lives on in infamy....the scheme didn't die with him.

This is a modern day Ponzi scheme as quoted from Crimes of Persuasion.

"A man who ran a $300 million Ponzi scheme has been indicted on charges of defrauding more than 500 people in 17 states. He promised to pay interest as high as 36% on investments in companies that make short-term, high-interest loans. Investors were told that the money would be invested in Cash 4 Titles and similar companies that provide high-interest loans to borrowers who pledge their car titles and future payroll checks as collateral.

Almost none of the investor funds went to Cash 4 Titles or to any other company engaged in providing 'car title loans' or making 'payroll check advances'. Instead, he used some of the money to pay off previous investors but transferred the bulk of it to an offshore account at the Bank of Bermuda.

Prosecutors are seeking the forfeiture of more than $25 million that he earned off the scheme, along with titles to his homes. They also seek forfeiture of the title and interest he held in a commercial aviation company.

A settlement between the Bank of Bermuda and victims of the Cayman-based Ponzi scheme received approval of the courts 10/12/01.

While continuing to deny liability, the settlement agreement provides for a payment of up to 50% of actual out of pocket losses to *investors in Cash 4 Titles, although the total payment, including all court approved fees and expenses, is not to exceed $67.5 million."*

Ponzi schemes really are crimes of persuasion and those who promote them can be called sneaky snakes. That is what they are.

The people who are duped into investing in such schemes aren't in any way planning to cheat of profit from another's misfortune. The investors are not criminals; they are victims.

A Ponzi scheme is comparable to pyramid scheme. You might even call it a very, very elaborate pyramid scheme.

Pyramid schemes aren't a new con game that was thought up by the sneaky snakes of the Internet. Pyramid schemes can be traced back to the 1950's when chain letters became very popular. You see rather harmless versions of pyramid schemes in your inbox occasionally. These emails will tell you that if you don't pass the email along to 10 or so of your closest friends, terrible things will happen to you but there is rarely any money involved.

The kind of pyramids that involve large sums of money are no longer sent through the USPS because they are very illegal and land those who send them in jail and have heavy fines levied against them.

Even if it wasn't illegal, it would be difficult to find enough people now days that would be willing to participate in such an obvious pyramid scheme. The public did finally become educated about pyramid schemes but that only served to make those who perpetrate them become better able to disguise them.

A real pyramid scheme never involves a real product. It involves money...not things...much like a Ponzi scheme.

An MLM scheme is also much like a Ponzi scheme or a pyramid scheme except that there is always a product involved in an MLM (Multi-Level Marketing) scheme.

The structure of an MLM scheme is a pyramid. The point is at the bottom and the structure grows larger as it progresses. Each 'layer' of the pyramid recruits the next layer which is larger than the one before it. Each layer is required to purchase inventory...this inventory is purchased from the underlying layer. Commissions are filtered down through the layers all the way to the bottom layer...or point. Eventually the pyramid collapses under its own weight. The top layer has the longest fall and stands to lose the most.

- Ponzi schemes are illegal.
- Pyramid schemes are illegal.
- MLM schemes are illegal.

The people who promote these schemes are some of the sneaky snakes that live and unfortunately thrive on the Internet but they aren't the only variety.

If you are out there doing business on the Internet you are visible. You are visible to your suppliers. You are visible to your customers. You are visible to your potential customers. You want to be visible to these people. You MUST be visible to these people. Sadly, you are also very visible to the sneaky snakes.

We've talked before about the **CAN-SPAM Act** and related rules and penalties but that doesn't mean that there aren't still spammers out there. There are laws against robbing convenience stores, too, but that still happens and so does SPAM.

These sneaky snake Spammers turn their spiders or robots loose to crawl through the Internet and harvest email addresses. Email addresses can be used many ways...one of them is identity theft.

You must make yourself available to your supplies, customers and potential customers but rather than post your email address on your website for the world to see...and the Spam spiders to find...it is better to embed your address in a graphic or to use contact information that is web based and does not publish your email address.

Another thing that email addresses that are collected by the Spam spiders are used for is to appeal to your generosity and your willingness to help those who are less fortunate than you. Great qualities...but ones that can be used by sneaky snakes to relieve you of some of your hard earned dollars. Here is a typical ploy and one that has been repeated for years:

Hello, my dear Friend,

Please excuse me for any inconvience caused by this message. My name is Valentin. I'm a student and I live with my mother in city Kaluga, Russia. My mother is invalid. She cannot see and she receive a very small pension which is not enough even for medications and food. I work very hard every day to be able to buy the necessities for my mother, but my salary is very small, because my studies still not finished. Due to deep crisis authorities stoped gas supply in our district and we cannot heat our home anymore. I don't know what to do, because the weather will be very cold in the next months and the temperature outside can be lower than minus 35 degrees Celsius, as it was in the last winter. I am very afraid that the temperature inside our home can be very cold and we will not be able to survive. I don't know what I can do in this situation.

Thanks to the free internet access in our local library I found several e-mail addresses and I decided to appeal to you with a prayer in my heart for a small help. If you have any old sleeping bag, warm blanket, portable stove, warm clothes and shoes, electric water-boiler, canned and dried food, vitamins, medicines from cold, any hygiene-products, I will be very grateful to you if you could send it to our postal address which is: Valentin Mikhailine, Rileewa Uliza, 6-45.Kaluga. 248030, Russia.

If you think that it would be better or easier for you to help with some money, please write me back and I will give you details for sending it safely if you agree. This way to help is very good because in this case I will be able to buy a portable stove and heat our home during the winter. I hope to hear from you very soon and I pray that you will be able to help us to survive this winter. I also hope very much that this hard situation will get better very soon in our country.

Please excuse me, once more, for any inconvience caused by this message.

Valentin and my mother Elena.

Kaluga.

Russia.

E-mail: valyam@eposte.ru

This is a hoax! It is a cruel one that is being repeatedly perpetrated by an Internet sneaky snake. I did not correct the spelling nor did I correct the grammar. This is exactly as it was received via email.

Then the emails that are harvested by the Spam spiders can also be used to send emails that are designed to appeal to your desire to make a lot of money without having to do any work...and be doing a good deed in the process. Wow! That sounds like a real win/win/win situation. It isn't....stop drooling.

This email is sent to you by somebody in a foreign country that has a lot of money or access to a lot of money and is concerned about crooked government officials getting their hands on his (or his family's or his church's) money.

All the sender of this email wants, he says, is to be allowed to use your bank account to protect the money from these crooked government officials...sometimes the money is meant for orphans or building a church or some other noble cause. In return for you allowing him to use your bank account, he will give you a substantial percentage of the funds just for your 'inconvenience'. This substantial percentage is often times said to be in the millions of dollars.

You may have heard of the Nigerian scam...that is hardly new news. But now there is one going around with a slightly different twist. This sneaky snake wants to give you back the money that his countrymen stole from you.....

Comment:gooddaysir/ma,

my name is usman abdulahi i am the chairman of the financial aid in nigeria.

my aiim of writting this lettrer is to inform you that thje rate which nigerians has been sending scam mail is much and has also been collecting money from people in other countries. we are sending this lettrer to every body who has nigerians must have stolen their money to please send us a mail and the information on how they collected yoiur money and the money will be sent to you.

the number of 1000 m,en has been caught running scams and has been arrested .we also went further on and saw the sum of $32million in their account and now this money has to be shared to every body who has lost their .i want you to send me a mail; if your was stollen so that we refund the money to you and also send us full information on how they collected it .i am expecting to hear from you to refund

thanks

usman abdulahi

Gee, I don't know....maybe if he could spell? Please....do NOT send your information to the sneaky snake. You can bet that the only thing you have to lose is some more money.

Do you know what the terms 'pharming and phishing' mean in Internet jargon? If you don't you need to know.

"Phishing is e-mail fraud where the perpetrator sends out legitimate-looking e-mails that appear to come from well known and trustworthy Web sites in an attempt to gather personal and financial information from the recipient. A phishing expedition, like the fishing expedition it's named for, is a speculative venture: the phisher puts the lure hoping to fool at least a few of the prey that encounter the bait."

The best prevention for a phishing scam is to never, EVER click on a link supplied by the sender of an email. It is wiser to always go to the site using either a bookmarked link of typing the address that you know to be legitimate into the address bar on your browser.

Many very reliable sites have been fooled be these snakes...big ones like Yahoo and Paypal. You can be fooled as well.

This definition was found on Wikipedia:

"Pharming is a scamming practice in which malicious code is installed on a personal computer or server, misdirecting users to fraudulent Web sites without their knowledge or consent. Pharming has been called "phishing without a lure."

Both of these illegal practices are used by the Internet sneaky snakes. They are designed to rob you of your personal information or to hack into your website.

We will discuss the problem of pharming a bit more in the next chapter.

Chapter 7
Watch Out for the Cannibals

Once you have ventured far enough into the Internet jungle, encountered and successfully survived meeting several lions, tigers, bears and sneaky snakes, the next thing you have to worry about are the (gasp!) cannibals!

When you first meet a cannibal, he will look, speak and act just like any other normal Internet business person. There won't be a bone stuck through his nose. He won't be carrying a spear or poison darts. He will be carrying....are you ready for this?......Software! That's right....I said...Software.

These cannibals have a particular fondness for newbies. They are easier marks than those who have been successfully living and thriving in the Internet jungle for awhile. Newbies aren't near as apt to ask the right questions before being bullied into purchasing software.

I'm sorry to say that newbies easily become software junkies. The become addicted to the stuff. If you show a newbie a piece of software that promises to lighten his work load or make him more successful or make his computer run better or faster, he is almost always interested. The Cannibals know this....they depend on it.

You, as a newbie, must recognize your software addiction and try to control it. It can not only cost you a ton of money, it can be downright dangerous.

Do you know what the acronym TUS stands for? You don't? I'll tell you. It stands for **T**otally **U**seless **S**oftware (TUS)...and the jungle is full of cannibals pushing it.

You DO need some software programs...there isn't any doubt about it. For example: You must have some kind of word processing program on your computer. The software that supplies this word processing ability, however, can be so bloated with un-needed features that all it does is eat up your computer resources. You will have paid a lot of bucks out for features that you do not need now and will most likely never need. The basic software is useless but the glut of added features makes most of it totally useless.

You can spend a lot of money on software that just simply won't help you to achieve your goals. You can even spend real hard-earned money on such foolishness as singing happy faces....no kidding.

You can buy software that will supply you with line charts, graphs, pie charts, etc. that have absolutely no discernible use. They might look really impressive but they don't mean anything.

But, hey, you might like a lava lamp icon on your task bar. Or, maybe you believe that there is software out there that can keep the evil spirits from invading your computer. If you do, maybe you should consider another line of work.

Besides TUS there are cannibals that will try to sell you pirated software. Everybody loves a bargain! There are no two ways about it...deep discounts are very, very attractive. This is another thing that the cannibals are well aware of.

Many very useful and needed pieces of software are often pirated. Programs like Adobe Photoshop or Microsoft Word are particularly vulnerable. It is illegal to sell pirated software but it is equally illegal to buy pirated software if you can reasonably believe that it has been pirated or stolen.

Here are a list of things that can help you determine if the jungle cannibals are trying to sell stolen software:

1. Check the price of the software on the website of the manufacturer. If the price that you are being offered is way out of line with what the manufacturer is charging, it is a pretty safe bet that you are being asked to buy stolen software. Don't.

1. If you agree to buy a piece of software...the price seems to be in line...but you get to the seller's sales and service page and are asked to forego your right to a chargeback claim on your credit card, do not complete the sale. You should always have the right to protest a sale and you never want to give up that right.

1. Each manufacturer of a legitimate software product places an embedded code in the software. You are very likely being asked to purchase stolen software if you are instructed to use a special number or a

different procedure to activate the software.

1. If you buy a piece of software and are sent a disc to install it on your computer and on the disc you see either NFR or OEM, it was stolen. NFR means, Not For Resale. This is most often stamped on a beta product version. OEM means Original Equipment Manufacturer. This code is stamped on software that is included in the purchase of a new computer.

1. All legitimate software can be registered. If the seller of the software tells you that it cannot be registered, you can bet that it was stolen. You are not a criminal but if you buy software that you know has been stolen, you can become a criminal. Receiving stolen property is a crime in all fifty states and in most civilized countries in the world. Don't!
2. Those who sell legitimate software will always supply you with their names, addresses and telephone numbers. They have nothing to hide. Those who are selling stolen or pirated software will not provide you with their real names, real addresses or real telephone numbers....and their email addresses are changed daily...or more frequently.

1. All legitimate software manufacturers and retailers will give you a written warranty. They will also have a very fair refund policy. The crooks will offer neither.

1. We've discussed what SPAM is. It is a bulk email that

> you receive that you have not asked for. Legitimate software manufacturers and retailers do not engage in the illegal act of sending SPAM. If you get an offer for a piece of software at a ridiculously low price and that offer arrives in your inbox as SPAM. Hit the delete button and forget about it.

If you order a piece of software at a really low price, pay for it, and it never shows up in your mail box or you don't receive the download instructions forthwith, that is the best of the bad things that can happen to you.

In the last chapter we talked about phishing and pharming briefly. Bogus software or stolen software or Totally Useless Software is the preferred method of cannibals to have you for lunch. These pieces of software very often contain malicious codes for the purpose of either phishing or pharming.

If you go to a website where bogus software is being sold, put in your personal information (including your credit card information), you will have been the victim of a phishing scam. Do you want to try to guess what will happen to that information that you supplied while you were looking for such a bargain? It won't be good, I can tell you that. You won't know who has your information or what they are going to do with it.

Pharming can be accomplished by these cannibals by embedding information into a disc or a download that can accomplish their evil plans for you. You can find that your computer no longer does what you tell it to do...you can be redirected to sites that can take information right out of your hard drive and then use it in any way they want to.

The bottom line of all this information is, that, yes, you do need software. Software makes the computers go round. It's what allows you to be creative and productive. BUT...you need no more than you NEED and that needs to be purchased from the manufacturers or from legitimate retailers even if you do have to pay more for it.

It is easy to become a software junkie. There is, after all, some really cool software out there and software is what makes your computer of more useful. The good software makes you better able to produce the work that you must produce in order to be a successful online employee or a successful online business owner. We all need software.

Before you actually purchase any software, however, you need to ask yourself three questions and you need to answer yourself honestly:

1. Is this piece of software something that I actually need? If the software will provide you with the ability to do your required work faster or make your job easier, then it is good software for you. If all the software is going to do is take up resources on your computer and slow it down without providing any real benefits for you, then it is TUS (Totally Useless Software). If the software is bloated with features that you will never use, you should look for a simpler or even older version. Added features eat up resources and slow your computer down.

1. Is the price I am paying in line with the prices charged by the manufacturer or legitimate retailers of

this software? This really is important. Receiving stolen goods is a crime.

1. Think of it like this: If someone offered to sell you a Rolex watch for $29.95, you would immediately know that the watch was either not a real Rolex or that is was hotter than a two dollar pistol.

You wouldn't be foolish enough to spend $30 on a fake watch and you sure wouldn't want to be guilty of receiving stolen merchandise...so either way...you would walk away. That same thing is true of software. If the price is too low, the software is either bogus or hot.

1. Is there a sufficient satisfaction guarantee? There are those super-duper-60-day-wonder salesmen out there that pride themselves on being able to sell ice boxes to Eskimos. They will make wild promises or jump through hoops just to make a sale.

Don't get suckered in....read the fine print!

You should never buy any piece of software that does not come with a guarantee. This guarantee should cover more than the fact that the software will work...it should also guarantee that if the software doesn't work for YOU that you can return it and get your money back.

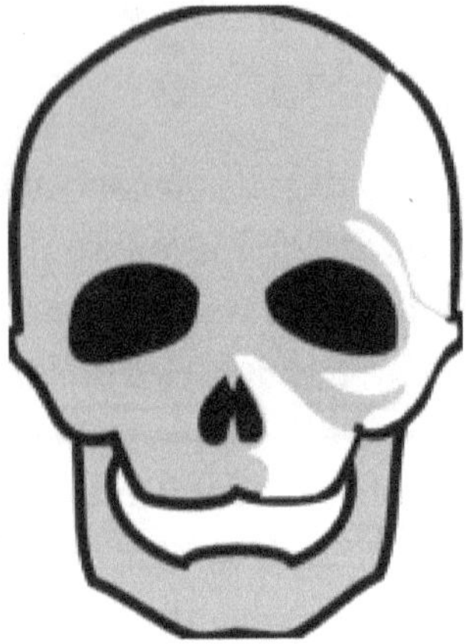

Chapter 8

There are Poisonous Plants

Besides lions, tigers, bears, oh my and sneaky snakes and cannibals, the jungle is overrun by vegetation....much of it is harmless but some of it can cause you or your computer to itch, brake out in hives or even be fatal if it's consumed.

You see, those of us who venture into the Internet commerce jungle are all hungry when we start. We are hungry for success. We either want our own businesses or we want jobs that we can do from home. That's why we are here...we are hungry!

You aren't the first Internet business jungle adventurer and you don't have to make all of the mistakes yourself. You can learn from the mistakes others, who have preceded you, have made and avoid them yourself. This information can save you a lot of stress and, yes, pain.

Some of these jungle plants look so innocent. They can even be beautiful and have such great appeal. They give off a heady perfume that smells like money.... money that can be made easily and quickly. They practically reek of success!

These plants can be so hypnotic that you can very easily be tempted into trying them. Money! Success! It is what every person who steps into the Internet business jungle is searching for and there is money and success growing in abundance right before your eyes...all you have to do is reach out and gather as much as you want....right? WRONG! Don't touch these fierce jungle plants!

Plants that Make You Itch

The HYIP Plant: This one has long stems that can reach out and grab you. HYIP is an acronym that means **H**igh **Y**ield **I**nvestment **P**rogram. There are two HYIP varieties.

> The first is a perfectly legal one. Many people who have the desire and the financial wherewithal to invest in an HYIP do so. They do so with both eyes wide open. They are well aware of the risks involved and those are risks that they are willing (and can afford) to take.

>

Legal HYIP's usually invest in such things as commodities and futures. There can be a potential of earning as much as a 3% return per DAY on an investment in a legitimate HYIP.

However, you must remember that high yield always carries an equally high risk. There is the potential for earning a large return but there is also the very real possibility of losing the total investment as well.

The legal HYIP variety that grows in the Internet jungle, as well as in the real brick and mortar world, presents opportunities and risks.

If you are really a born gambler and you can financially afford to lose your investment, legal HYIP's might be a reasonable choice for you to make.

› The illegal HYIP: This insidious plant grows wild in the Internet jungle. It releases an odor of easy money that is intoxicating to unwary adventurers.

The illegal HYIP is very much like the legal variety except that the yield promised is much, MUCH higher and the time of return expected is much, MUCH shorter.

Even the Federal Bureau of Investigation (FBI) has warned about such illegal HYIP schemes. You can read all of the details of the FBI warning by clicking here[1]. In part the FBI says:

"The purpose of this notice is to alert the public to persons who have reportedly marketed investment schemes which appear to be fraudulent. Various "prime bank" trading programs, or similar trading programs which purport to offer above average market returns with below market risk through the trading of bank instruments are fraudulent.

1. http://www.quatloos.com/FBI_warning_HYIP.htm

> Offering such programs, or claiming to be able to introduce investors to persons who have access to such programs, violates numerous federal laws, including
>
> criminal laws."
>
> Whoa! That sounds serious! The FBI report goes on describe the details of these illegal HYIP's.

All HYIP's are based on speculation...both the legal and illegal varieties. If you choose to invest in an HYIP, you need to be aware that what you are investing in is a building that hasn't been built or a product that hasn't been launched or the educated guess of a person or organization that is in the position to make such and educated guess. You are BETTING that other people will succeed in a prospective financial venture.

***Note:** Legitimate HYIP's do not send unsolicited emails. If you receive an offer to invest your money in a HYIP via unsolicited email...it IS the illegitimate variety.

The Intermediary Plant: This plant usually sprouts up as an unsolicited "opportunity" in your inbox. That, all by itself, should raise red flags for you. Remember that big opportunities that are real and legitimate are not sent by unsolicited bulk email...that is SPAM. Real big opportunities are very, VERY rare if they exist at all. I've never personally seen one.

The offer will always be from someone that you do not know and will usually have a name that sounds 'foreign'. It will NOT address you by name...that is another little tip off that you are looking at a poisonous intermediary plant.

It will usually begin with a formal greeting such as, 'Good Day'. The following is a copy of a real unsolicited email that made the rounds back in 2004 as reported by Snopes[2]:

"Good day, my name is Evaldas Vytautas.

I'm Sales Manager of Lionder Web Design Agency. We are situated in Vilnius, Lithuania.

Lionder Web Design Agency is pleased to offer you the position of Exchange Manager for our organization. We are excited about the potential that you bring to our company.

We work with corporate clients and some of them prefer to do wire transfers, however we cannot receive international wire transfers because of heavy taxes. Tax for international wire transfer is 25% In Lithuania. There is no sense for us to work in such a way, however we don't want to lose our clients. You need to have Paypal/bank account. System is completely automated. You will work only 1-2 hours a day, receive, process payments from our clients through your Paypal/bank account. Report about all new payments, act only within the limits of law — earn minimum $1500-$2000 per month.

Your salary will be 5-15% from every processed amount (you begin from 5%).

To join the minimum requirements include :

-MINIMUM QUALIFICATIONS (Skills, Knowledge, Ability, etc.)

-The minimum qualifications are diploma or equivalent.

-Must be able to multi-task and have good communication skills.

-Knowledge of MS Word and other basic computer programs.

-This being a new field there is NO experience needed.

---

2. http://www.snopes.com/crime/fraud/reshipper.asp

HOW TO APPLY:

If you would like to pursue this opportunity simply send Your Resume (CV) to resume@lionder.net OR Download Job Application Form

(www.lionder.net/Job_Application_Form.doc), fill it in and send us to resume@lionder.net (No phone calls please. Callers will not be considered for the position).

We will respond promptly.

Please don't feel shy to contact our Online Support and ask any questions you will have:

Contact Name: Julie Jakulyte

ICQ- 257235542,

AOL IM Screen Name- Jakulyte,

Yahoo! ID: JJakulyte,

MSN- Jakulyte@hotmail.com.

No agencies, please.

Lionder Web Design Agency is an equal opportunity/ affirmative action employer.

For more information about who we are and what we do, please visit our webiste — www.lionder.net

It is necessary that we know your decision by November 20, 2004, so that we can plan accordingly.

Regards,

Evaldas Vytautas

Lionder Web Design Agency"

This intermediary plant was designed specifically to attract those who are searching for a work-at-home job. It was sent well after the enactment of **CAN-SPAM**...so a little thing like it being against the law to send SPAM does NOT stop these plants from proliferating.

****NOTE!** It would be a very good idea for you to book mark or add to your favorites this link: http://www.snopes.com/ Snopes sniffs out and broadcasts all kinds of frauds and scams. Before you invest any money or even before you forward an email to your friends, you should always check the claims out on Snopes[3].com.

The SSS Plant: I made that acronym up....it refers to the secret shopped scam but it is a plant that flourishes in the Internet jungle. Who doesn't like to shop? The idea of shopping with other people's money and getting PAID to do it is a big temptation. You would really like to pick armloads of that plant, wouldn't you? Wait!

Secret shopper 'jobs' come in two varieties. There is the legitimate variety and the illegal variety...or the scam. It is very difficult to tell the varieties apart. They can appear side by side in the classified ad pages of a newspaper or on work-at-home job websites.

One very certain way to tell some of the illegal plants are that legitimate secret shopper jobs will never require you to purchase training supplies or courses to teach you have to do the job. The problem is that some of the illegal ones don't require that you make purchases either but knowing that the legal ones NEVER do will help to eliminate at least some of the wrong choices.

The better of the bogus secret shopper job offers are only out to sell you useless training supplies or courses with no job attached. The worst of the secret shopper job offers are to get you to make illegal purchases or to ship illegal goods or to act

---

3. http://www.snopes.com/

as a middle man for illegal fund transfers.....all of which can get you into some very serious legal difficulties.

The advertisements for secret shopper jobs are made to sound very enticing. They promise that you can make large sums of money by working only a very few hours each week. They assure you that there are no educational requirements and no experience that will be required. These promises make these advertisements look like answered prayers to those who are desperate for a job and have little or no experience and a limited educational background.

Those who answer these advertisements will often receive a check in the amount of several thousand dollars with instructions to get the check cashed either at their personal bank or at a bank that is designated. Then they are to purchase a money order for the amount of the check less the cost of the money order and a hundred dollars or so that they can keep. The money order is to be made payable to a person that they have never heard of but whom they must say is a relative. The money order then must be mailed to an address (usually a Post Office Box) in Canada or some other country.

It is what is called money laundering...and the secret shopper who participates in the scheme is now part of the illegal act. Not only will they have committed an illegal act but they may well have paid for that privilege.

Here is the free advice that is offered to those seeking secret shopper jobs by the Federal Trade Commission (FTC):

"The truth is that it is unnecessary to pay money to anyone to get into the mystery shopper business. The shopping certification offered in advertising or unsolicited email is almost always worthless. A list of companies that hire mystery shoppers is available for free; and legitimate mystery shopper jobs are on the Internet for free. Consumers who try to get a refund from promoters of mystery shopping jobs usually are out of luck. Either the business doesn't return the phone calls, or if it does, it's to try another pitch."

The Forwarding Plant: This plant (also known as the 'forwarding-e-mail') grows wild in the Internet jungle. It has been around a long time. Many have tried to eradicate it and yet it thrives. There are dozens of varieties.

The very idea of being able to make money, get paid for vacations or great merchandise by simply forwarding emails sounds very enticing to those who are not all that computer savvy. It sounds easy and it sound quick and it sounds like something that they already know how to do....forward.

The problem is that the technology doesn't even exist for email tracking. Another tiny little problem is that nobody is going to pay you or anybody else for forwarding emails...it hasn't happened...it isn't happening...and it will NEVER happen.

Please take note....you will NOT receive:

› Cash from Microsoft

› Free Merchandise from Nike

› Free clothing from Gap

› $25 Gift Certificates from Abercrombie & Fitch, Old Navy, or Outback Steakhouse

› Free cars from Honda

> Free Cases of coke from Coca Cola

> Or anything else

By forwarding emails! It isn't going to happen! Let me tell you what you WILL get if you choose to pick this plant. You will get a lot of very unhappy recipients of forwarded email. Forward enough of these things and you could be facing an angry lynch mob made up of a few hundred of your nearest and dearest friends! ☺

The World Currency Plant: It seems that unless you were a couple of cans short of a six pack, this would be an obviously poisonous plant and one that you would avoid.

This is another of those plants that you usually first see when it sprouts up in your inbox as an unsolicited bulk email....do you see a pattern here? SPAM is always, always, ALWAYS offers and opportunities that are bogus and downright dangerous!

The world currency cartel plant looks a lot like a cactus plant that has gone wild. It will be a very long letter filled with large blocks of text that you won't be inclined to read.

> It will not address you by your name but rather as 'Dear Friend' or some other such generic salutation.

> There will be a lot of 'testimonials'. We've discussed testimonials before. Remember? Anybody can write a testimonial and type anybody else's name as the author. Just because there is a testimonial from a person whose name you recognize, does

NOT mean that they actually wrote that testimonial.

› In a few thousand carefully chosen words, the letter will tell you that you can make boat loads of money by only making one little telephone call for each 'transaction'.

Say, WHAT???? You can make tons of money by doing nothing more strenuous than making an occasional phone call? You have GOT to be kidding!

Well...actually they aren't trying to be funny....they are trying to get into your bank account. They usually only want 35 of YOUR dollars but they are planning on taking $35 out of many, many bank accounts. You are just one of many that they are offering to share this incredible money making secret with. Save your 35 bucks....making money is a little harder than making a phone call.

The UWON Plant: How strange! You are notified that you have won the lottery and you didn't even buy a ticket. How lucky is THAT? Not only did you win the lottery, you won it in a foreign country that you have never even visited!

This plant thrives mostly on greed and gullibility. News flash! You can't win a lottery if you haven't bought a ticket. Lottery winners are selected according to numbers they choose when they PAID to enter a lottery.

You can find details on the Snopes[4] website. The gist of this scam is that you will need to send anywhere from $300

4. http://www.snopes.com/crime/fraud/lottery.asp

to $2000 in order to collect the millions that are owed to you because you won a lottery...a lottery that you didn't enter.

Chapter 9

All the Natives Aren't Friendly

You are doing great! You are getting close to being at the very heart of this Internet jungle and you have survived lions, tigers, bears, oh my and sneaky snakes, cannibals and poisonous plants to boot. You are learning to live and thrive in this jungle.

By this time you have likely met some of the natives. Most of them are nice, polite, helpful people. You have even come to be friends with some of them. You might even have formed, in not friendships, at least relationships with some of your toughest competitors. That isn't the least bit uncommon out here in the Internet jungle.

It's been said that, 'Politics makes strange bedfellows', it could be said that the Internet makes for even stranger bedfellows! You may have seen joint venture agreements made between fierce competitors who sell the very same products to the very same market. It happens. When the details of a joint venture agreement can be worked out so that each partner can equally benefit from that agreement, joint venture agreements between competitors are not all that uncommon.

It is also true that there really are gurus that live and work in the Internet jungle. These living, breathing gurus are real experts in their internet marketing fields of endeavor.

There are experts in article and ebook writing and marketing. There are experts in viral marketing techniques. There are experts in the writing of effective sales letters. There are many real experts or gurus that often offer courses, seminars, teleseminars and webinars in order to teach those who can pay for the information how to do certain things and do them very well in the Internet marketing jungle.

There are Fake Gurus

However, just because somebody claims to be a guru or an expert doesn't make them a real guru or expert. Sometimes that claim just makes them another one of the not-so-friendly jungle natives.

The think about signing up for courses, seminars, teleseminars or webinars is that there is not recourse to getting your money back if all you get is a bunch of stuff that anybody would know who had been in the Internet marketing arena for more than fifteen minutes.

You can't say, 'They didn't tell me anything I didn't already know. I want my money back" and expect to get your money back. That isn't going to happen.

The best thing that you can do before you sign up for any instruction is to check out the instructors or speakers who will be presenting information to you. Run a check on them by plugging their names into the Google search box. This won't tell you everything you need to know, but it is a place to start.

Ask other marketers if they know who these so-called experts or gurus are and if they have ever taken a course or attended a seminar, teleseminar or webinar where these same gurus or experts were the instructors or speakers.

Who Make Fake Claims

Remember that anybody can CLAIM anything to be a fact...but that doesn't make it a real fact. An 'expert' can TELL you and the rest of the world that he charges $1000 to write a single 300-400 word article. Maybe he does CHARGE that...the question is whether there is anybody who actually PAYS him that much for a single article. It isn't likely.

Still he can claim that as a fact and offer to teach you how to write articles that you can charge $1000 each for. Of course, in order for him to teach you his wonderful article writing secrets, you will be required to pay him for this information and to pay him very dearly indeed. He needs it...he isn't making any money writing articles. He isn't one of the friendly natives.

P.S. You aren't going to make a thousand bucks for writing a single article. In order to make that 1000 bucks you are going to have to write a whole BUNCH of articles at about $4 or $5 each....if you are a very good writer, know the rules of Internet article writing and are very lucky.

Another common fake claim by Internet jungle natives who are of the not-so-friendly variety, is the 'I'm making boat loads of money'. They CLAIM that they are making...oh I don't know....$100,000 a MONTH by using their fool-proof money making system.

Remember....anybody can CLAIM anything as a fact. There are a lot of things that can slip past the 'Truth in Advertising Act' in the Internet marketing jungle.

Okay...think about that for just a minute. If they were in fact making $100,000 each and every month with their fool proof money making system, why is it, do you suppose that they are willing to teach you (and anybody else that has the price of a ticket) how to compete with them? If you had found out how to locate the pot of gold at the end of every rainbow, would you sell that information at any price? I don't think so.

The 'claim to fame by association' is another one of the ploys used by these unfriendly natives. They claim that they are associated with some of the real gurus of Internet marketing or that they have very close personal relationships with famous or powerful people and that association makes the information that they are attempting to sell you very, VERY valuable.

They do not claim that they actually have the credentials that make themselves gurus but they are associated with people who are true gurus or are in a position to open doors or influence people on your behalf.

Now I am not saying that knowing influential people isn't an asset. It certainly is. It is not, however, much of an asset to 'know someone who knows someone'. That certainly isn't a privilege worth paying for.

And Wild Promises

Have you ever seen those crazy advertisements for seminars or courses that say something like, "I guarantee you that I can teach you how to get the number one spot in Google search results!" That one really makes me want to laugh!

It's all in the way an advertisement is worded, folks. You were NOT promised that you would actually HAVE the number one spot in Google search results....only that you would be taught how to GET the number one spot in Google search results.

I can teach you that right now in only one sentence. Get more clicks and have more links on the Internet than your competitors. That's pretty much it. The trick is HOW to get more clicks than your competitors and HOW to get more links on the Internet than your competitors. The devil is always in the details....those pesky little details!

There are many tried and true techniques to raise your PR (Page Rank) but even when you know what all of those techniques are and are diligently applying all of them, the odds against getting being number one in search results fall somewhere between one and a snowball's chance in hell.

Page Rank is one of those things that you can just mention to a very seasoned, very well-established REAL marketing guru and cause him to begin to drool uncontrollably. It's what everybody works for and what everybody dreams of.

A Page Rank of 7 is considered to be practically sacred ground. Nobody...but NOBODY can ever guarantee to make you number one. Don't believe it! Don't buy into it!

Yes, you do need to learn all of the techniques and how to use them to increase your visibility on the Internet. That information is actually available for free if you are willing to look for it.

If you aren't willing or are unable to seek out the free information on the Internet, you can take courses, attend seminars, teleseminars or webinars that are given by legitimate gurus on article and ebook writing and marketing, posting to blogs and forums, banner exchanges, joint ventures and other techniques that can be used to help you raise your page rank and your visibility. None of these legitimate gurus will ever promise to teach you how to be number one. They know better.

Yet another wild promise that some of the unfriendly Internet jungle natives will make is, "I will teach you how to get lucrative joint venture deals!" Hmmm....well there really are lucrative joint venture deals out there on the Internet. There isn't any doubt about THAT fact....you getting them is another story.

You will notice that the advertisement doesn't say that you will in fact HAVE a lucrative joint venture deal if you take the course or whatever is being offered. It only says that this (maybe) guru will teach you HOW to get one for yourself.

The phrase, joint venture, is another one that causes well-established Internet marketers as well as brand new Internet marketers to get all shivery and weak in the knees. Everybody knows that a joint venture is the fastest and easiest way to make a lot of money, build a large opt-in list, to get established or become better established in the Internet jungle.

Like high search engine rankings, joint ventures are the darlings of the Internet jungle. They are the gold rings....the prizes most sought after....something everybody wants.

You can get a joint venture. I am not saying that this is a prize that is out of your reach now or that will always be out of your reach. I AM saying that getting a joint venture deal is almost as easy as catching that golden ring on the merry-go-round was when you were a child. It can be done...but not without a lot of stretching and practice.

Here are the hard cold facts about getting your first joint venture. In order to get an established Internet marketer to join you in a joint venture, you will most likely have to give him or her 100% of the profit on a product that you have produced or had produced for you. This product will have to have a value of at least $100 to attract a marketer who has a substantial opt-in list. The only thing that you will get out of your first joint venture, most likely, is a big increase in your own opt-in list.....which is very, VERY valuable but the bank won't credit it to your account.

Now, you do need to know how to approach established Internet marketers. You do need to know how to structure joint venture agreements and how to build squeeze pages whereby you capture the names and email addresses for your own opt-in list.

If you work hard, follow the rules and pay your dues, someday you will be that well established marketer who will GET 100% of the profits but it won't be today...or even next week.

They Will Offer to Show You the Shortcut

Have you ever noticed that every time you have ever tried to take a shortcut, it always ends up taking longer or costing you more money in the long run? It seems like that is always the way a shortcut works out...at least for me.

One of the shortcuts that these less-than-friendly natives will offer is a way to get an opt-in list with out having to do all of the heavy lifting. They say that they can show you a shortcut...a way to get an opt-in list the 'easy way'.

"Oh, no", they say. "You really don't have to offer a nice incentive. You don't have to do all that work.....like writing and marketing articles and ebooks or posting to blogs and forums. There is an easier way....and I just happen to have it handy. For a small price it can be yours."

Since building an opt-in list really does involve a lot of 'heavy lifting' so to speak, you might well be tempted to take the shortcut that they are offering.

Here is a little piece of very good advice. Don't!

The shortcut they will be offering to show you for that 'very small' price is to BUY a list. You will see advertisements all over the Internet for companies who will sell you an opt-in list that they say contains names and email addresses of people who have already opted in....some of them twice.

The monetary cost of these lists is usually anywhere from 3 cents per name and email address on up to and about 30 cents per name and address. The price mostly depends on whether the lists contain names and addresses that are of the single opt-in variety or the double opt-in variety.

This is a tempting shortcut but it is also a situation where you need to take a deep breath, a giant step backward and take a good clear look at exactly what you will be getting if you buy a list.

Here's the very first question that you need to ask yourself. **How often do you opt-in to a list on a website...any website?** Is your answer:

Often?

Occasionally?

Very rarely?

Next Question: **Why do you opt-in to a list?**

(a) Because you want the incentive gift that is being offered?

(b) Because you want the information that you will receive?

(c) Because you are really fond of getting a lot of emails from people you don't know?

Final Question: **Why do you think other people opt-in to lists?**

a. They want the incentive gift that is being offered?

a. They want the information that they will receive?

a. They just really like getting lots of email from companies and individuals who are trying to sell them stuff?

The one thing that is important here is that opt-in lists are NOT made up of just names and email addresses. They are made up of real people who are very much like you. When emails are sent they are received in the inboxes of real honest-to-goodness live people.

Do you know a single solitary person who would deliberately allow their name and email address to be added to a list of names and email addresses that would be sold to anybody with the price to buy them? Me, either....and I know a few ditzy people...ditzy, yes, crazy, no.

A determined identity thief can get enough information with just a legitimate email address to accomplish his evil purpose. People know that. They do NOT give out their names and email addresses for the purpose of having them sold to others and they sure as heck don't agree to it TWICE!

Do you want to know who might well give out their names and email addresses knowing that they are to be sold to others? I can tell you that. They are members of CAN-SPAM watch dog groups or those who are deeply involved in consumer protection or who want to report spammers and possibly collect the rewards.

The fact is that there is absolutely no such thing as an opt-in list that you can buy. The people who opted in did not opt-in to YOUR list. They opted in to someone else's list.

Unless you can prove that the emails that you send are sent only to those people who have opted in to YOUR list, you are violating the CAN-SPAM act. Violations can cost you the big bucks.

Another shortcut that you might be offered by these Internet jungle natives is automated article submission soft ware. Now, let me be clear. Some of this automated article submission software can be of some help.

Submitting articles and ebooks to article banks and ebook repositories is one of the most time consuming of tasks. It is very tempting to look for a shortcut to this process

The biggest problem with using automated article submission software is that most of the major banks and repositories will not accept submissions that are made with such software. They require that each submission be made by hand and individually in order for them to be listed on their sites.

One more shortcut that may be pointed out to you by these not-so-helpful natives is FFA's. Usually the native that will be showing you this particular shortcut owns the FFA page.

Oh, wait a minute. Maybe you don't know what FFA means. FFA is an acronym that means '**F**ree **F**or **A**ll'. Whoa! Sounds like a lot of fun, doesn't it? It's not that kind of free for all.

An FFA is usually set up as a link on a website. On this page, anybody who wants to can put in an advertisement for their website (something like a classified ad)....supposedly for others to see, be impressed by and visit. That is not exactly what happens, however.

What really happens is that you have opted in to a list and your inbox is about to fill up to the point of overflow everyday into the distant future. The only positive thing that you will get out of this shortcut is one link for search engine spiders to count and the negative thing you will get is an inbox full of sales letters for everything from soup to hay.

Chapter 10
Go Well Armed

When you earn your living from your own home, on your personal computer that is connected to the Internet, you think of yourself as being in a safe place. The bad guys are all out there in the real world waiting to mug you on your way to a job in the brick and mortar world, right? Wrong.

When you connect your personal computer to the Internet, you will have just walked into a jungle that is fraught with dangerous animals and even more dangerous natives.

In order to successfully hold an online job or run your own online business, you need to be aware of the dangers that await you. That is what we have tried to do in this book.

However, staying safe, staying on the right side of the law and keeping your job or staying in business is really up to you. You know there are lions and tigers and bears, oh my. You know there are sneaky snakes, poisonous plants, cannibals and unfriendly natives. You know that there are many traps that can set, bait that can be used to entice you and shortcuts that aren't really shortcuts that will lead you to where you want to be.

So....as 'they' say, "The best offense is a good defense!" Your good defense consists of being well armed, well prepared and having a plan for success.

Arm Yourself with Knowledge

Zoning Laws

Before you even apply for your online job or start your online business, you need to know if you can legally work from your own home. The odds are, that if you are going to be working alone, you will most likely not be affected by zoning laws, restrictions of an owners association or a tenant agreement unless you plan to stock and ship merchandise or unless you plan to have employees working for you at your home.

If your job or your business plan is to simply work all by yourself using your home computer, you will not likely be violating any body else's space.

On the other hand, if you do plan to store inventory and ship merchandise or if you do plan on having employees working with you from your home, then you need to know what the local zoning laws are. You need to know if there are restrictions placed on you by an owner's association agreement that you signed or on a tenant agreement or lease that you signed.

You need to gather this information and educate yourself before you step into the Internet jungle. You don't want to get shut down before you even get started.

Tax Laws

You don't want the tax man to get you. There may well be local taxes that you will be responsible for and reports that you will need to file when you are working from or running a business from your home.

There could be state taxes, as well. If you are selling merchandise, even electronic merchandise, you may well be responsible for collecting and reporting sales tax. You need to know this before you sell your first item.

Sales tax is supposed to be collected from the buyer of the merchandise by the seller of the merchandise and then reported and paid by the seller to the state and/or local tax entities.

You WILL owe the sales tax whether you collected it or not. Your tax bill will include not only the tax you should have collected from your customers but additional fines and penalties as well.

When you are employed online, you most often work as a contractor. That is...you are self-employed. Your employer will not be paying in part of your FICA. You are working for yourself and you are responsible for reporting your income and paying your taxes.

Your employer will supply you with a W-9 form at the end of the tax year. This form will show you the total amount the employer paid you. A copy of this form is sent to the IRS. It will include your social security number. There will have been no deductions made from the wages that you were paid so you will have to file a self employment form with your income tax returns and pay all of your own social security tax yourself.

This percentage is at 15.3% now. You will be responsible for filing quarterly reports for estimated earnings and making deposits based on those estimates.

It is a very wise thing to keep good records of your earnings, as well as, your expenditures. You don't want to wait until it is time to file your taxes and find out that you need a lot more information than you have and you most certainly do not want to find yourself sitting across a desk from the dreaded tax man without being well armed with detailed and provable records.

Ignorance of the law has never been and never will be an acceptable excuse. Penalties and fine can be really stiff. Keep good records!

Hire or Buy Some Protection

You need to be sure that you have some protection in place....remember that good defense? Some new Internet employees and new Internet entrepreneurs got so involved in just getting a job or starting a business that they forget to hire or buy some protection.

You need good records. Good records are the very best defense for many situations that come up when you are working online or running an online business enterprise of any kind,

You certainly do need financial records. If you have no bookkeeping or accounting knowledge yourself, you will need to hire someone to keep financial records for you. The earlier you do this, the better off you will be. Don't wait until January to hire a bookkeeper or start your own bookkeeping records.

If you have any bookkeeping or accounting knowledge, you might be able to keep your own records by using Quickbooks[1] or a similar online or downloadable accounting program. There are free ones and Microsoft Money usually is included when you purchase a new computer.

1. http://quickbooks.intuit.com/

There are many different accounting programs out there. Some of them are lacking in features while others are overloaded with features that you don't need now and will most likely never need. Too much of a good thing just slows your computer down and drains the resources. Get as much as you need for your job or your online business but don't buy more than you need.

If you are not comfortable keeping your own financial records, you can hire others to do that task for you. You can hire a bookkeeper or an accountant in the real brick and mortar world in close proximity to your home or you can hire a bookkeeper or an accountant that lives and works on the Internet.

Besides financial records, there are other records that you need. You will need to set up files on your computer to store information and make it easy for you to find.

› You will need a file for your business contacts....names, addresses, phone numbers and email addresses.....the name of their companies, notes of telephone conversations, emails to them and from them, etc.

› You will need a file for your media contacts....names, addresses, phone numbers and email addresses.....the names of the radio or TV stations, newspapers or magazines they work for, telephone conversation notes, emails to and from them, etc.

› You will need a file for proposals you have sent.

› You will need a file for proposals you have received.

› You will need a file for contracts that you have entered into.

› You will need a file for articles and ebooks that you have written and submitted...who they were submitter to....the results of the submissions, etc.

There are many other files that you will need to set up and maintain on your computer according to the work you are doing or the business that you are engaged in.

If you use an instant message program, be sure that you save all business related conversations. This is an option that you must choose on most instant messaging programs.

You need a work scheduling program. If you are to succeed in the online jungle you must have a plan or attack! If you just haphazardly do whatever comes to mind next, you will find yourself unorganized and unproductive. There are many such work scheduling programs available on the Internet. Some of them are even free.

You may think that because you aren't required to punch a clock that it isn't necessary for you to have a schedule but you are wrong. The very fact that you don't have to punch a clock or answer to a boss is the very reason that making a schedule for yourself is doubly important.

You need a starting time, you need scheduled breaks and you need a quitting time. It's true that you can't always stick to a schedule but you need to have one and do the very best you can to keep yourself on it.

Many of these work scheduling programs come with a built-in 'to-do' list option. You do want that and you do want to use it. It is so very easy to get side-tracked when you are working at home. Staying focused and staying 'on-point' will make success come much easier and much faster.

Make Your Own Rules

Sometimes when you are making your way through the Internet jungle, it will appear to others that you are doing nothing more than sitting in front of your computer or talking on the telephone.

These other people are not the enemy....or at least they really don't mean to be the enemy. They are your family and your friends. They don't mean any harm but they can't see where you have a real job.

After all, you don't get up, get dressed, leave home, drive to a job and return home in the evening. They assume that you are unemployed and just amusing yourself on your computer.

This leads them to believe that you obviously have time on your hands and should be available to run errands for others, talk to them on the telephone or have a pot of coffee ready and be yearning for their company at any time of the day.

This is a problem that is closely related to scheduling your work except that is scheduling your working DAY. You need to lay down specific rules, make them perfectly clear to your family and friends and provide visual clues to them.

By 'visual clues' I mean that you need a specific work space....a separate room that is your home office would be the best...one with a door that can be closed and a separate telephone line that is only for business. If that isn't possible, then a corner of a room that is used for other things but that has a door that can be closed can work. Have that business telephone line installed just as soon as you can swing it financially.

Your work day schedule should have:

- A starting time
- Scheduled lunch and coffee break times
- A quitting time

When you are working your way through the internet jungle, you need to be totally focused on not only surviving but on thriving.

Each evening when you have yet again outwitted the lions, tigers, bears, etc, you should have your full attention focused on your family, your friends, your hobbies, etc.

We can all get put into positions where one world must overlap the other. Those things happen but you need to keep the two worlds as separate as you can. You will also need to put a lid on your guilt complex if you have one. You are NOT a terrible person because you can't take 3 hours out of your day to take old Aunt Mae to her beauty shop appointment. Everybody else is working? So are you! Get over it....other arrangements can be made.

You might need to stand in front of a mirror and practice saying, "No" and saying it effectively.

Recognize Real Opportunity

It's easy to get so aware of the dangers out in the internet business jungle that you fail to recognize real opportunities when they present themselves.

Remember this....all of the natives are not UNFRIENDLY and there are some cannibals that feed on the bad guys only. Along with lions, tigers, bears and snakes there are also helpful creatures. There are plants that are medicinal, too.

Danger and opportunity live side by side in the Internet business jungle. You just need to be able to tell the difference between the two. You don't want to fall into a trap or get eaten alive but neither do you want to miss out on the real and vibrant opportunities that also abound.

To help yourself recognize opportunity and avoid danger in the internet business jungle, ask yourself these questions:

Is it legal?

In order to answer this question about any situation you are presented with, whether it be entering into a business agreement or buying a piece of software, you need to know what the laws are and what the rules and regulations are that govern the specific situation. Knowing the laws, rules and regulations makes you strong and able to recognize a real opportunity when it happens.....they DO happen!

Is it real?

There is so much hype out there that is sometimes very difficult to get past the hype and down to the bear facts of an offer. Ignore the super duper salesmen and look hard and long at the product, service or offer itself. Only you can determine what is real and what is just fluff, hype and a polished sales spiel.

Will it help me?

Whether you are thinking about taking a seminar, teleseminar or webinar or buying a piece of software, agreeing to a business arrangement or hiring a bookkeeper or a consultant, ask yourself if it will really help you get to where you are going.

Educate Yourself

Everybody knows something that you don't know. It might be what TO do or it might be what NOT to do....but everybody knows something. It's been said, 'Get and education'. You have probably had that preached to you since you were knee high to a duck. It's good advice but what nobody tells you is that you ARE getting an education....of some kind. We all get an education just by living in this world.

Of course, you were being told to get a formal education...go to school....go to college....get advanced degrees. It's not bad advice but that isn't the only way to become educated.

When you make your plans for either getting an online job or starting an online business, you need to start educating yourself. You need to set aside a certain amount of time each and every day to learn something that you need to know....something that will help you reach your goals...something about the niche that you are concentrating on.

Knowledge is power! Knowledge makes surviving and thriving in the Internet jungle possible.

Plan Your Jungle Adventure

There is an anonymous quote that is frequently used. "Those who fail to plan, plan to fail." It sounds trite but it is very accurate.

A business plan is not important...it is vital to achieving any measure of success. It is much like a road map. You wouldn't think about taking off on a cross country road trip without a road map.

The first thing that you need to determine when you are making your business plan is where you are now, what your assets are, and what your ultimate destination is. If you don't know where you are going, how will you know when you get there? This ultimate destination is your long range goal. Write it down.

Then you take that information and you plan the small steps that will be required to get from Point A to Point B. The journey will not be accomplished with a few giant steps but rather with many baby steps. Write them down, too.

Find a Jungle Guide

Having a map is great...having a guide is better. Having both a map AND a guide will almost guarantee that you will arrive at your destination without taking a lot of detours and side trips.

A jungle guide....a mentor....can be your strongest asset. If you know where you are and where you want to be, a mentor can show you the quickest and most direct path by which to get there.

Often times well-seasoned and well established Internet marketers, gurus and experts will take a newbie under their wing, so to speak, and guide them in making good business decisions....lead then down the right path.

You would do well to actively look for such a guide...a mentor. Ask questions and then listen for the answers. Take the advice of those who have already made all of the mistakes and are willing to help you avoid the same pitfalls and prevent you from falling into the same traps.

Chapter 11
Go Well Prepared

You are almost ready to begin your big adventure or to continue your big adventure better equipped and better armed. You are going to succeed!

Let's just double check the supplies and be certain that you have what is necessary. Here is a check list of what is required to successfully survive and thrive in the Internet jungle:

1. **An Itinerary**: You know where you are. You know where you want to be. You have made a good and doable business plan that will get you there. Check!

2. **Information:** You have this information:

› **You know about the wild animals:** You understand that there are lions, tigers, bears and sneaky snakes out there in the jungle and you are prepared to either avoid them or overcome them. Check!

› **You can identify poisonous plants:** There are evil plants that thrive in the Internet jungle and there are medicinal plants that help you to survive. You can now identify all the varieties. Check!

› **You know what baits are used in traps:** You can spot a trap and identify the bait in it without getting caught. Check!

› **You know which natives are friendly:** You can easily identify a cannibal or just an unfriendly native. You can, also, identify friendly and helpful natives. Check!

1. **Help:** You know where to go to look for help as you travel through the Internet jungle.

› You know how to use a search engine to check out the validity of people as well as facts.

› You know that attending real brick and mortar seminars that are being conducted by real (not fake) experts can help you in many ways. You will meet those who can help you in person.

4. **Supplies:** You should have ample quantities of these supplies:

› **Ambition:** Success in the Internet jungle depends a great deal on the desire of the adventurer. Unless you want to secure a better life for yourself and for your family, your success is in jeopardy. Check!

› **Determination:** A very large supply is required. You will be using your determination supply to keep yourself going when it looks like nothing is happening. Check!

› **Work Ethic:** You need a really strong one. You must be willing to work as long and as hard as you need to in order to accomplish your goals. This work ethic must be strong enough to keep you from succumbing to taking 'shortcuts' that will, in the end, turn out to be long cuts. Check!

› **Time:** You will need a lot of this....be sure to pack plenty. You are going to have to forego many pleasures in order to be able to spend enough time on your work-at-home job or your at-home business. Don't believe anybody who tells you that you can make plenty of money by just working part time. Check!

› **Hard Work:** You must be willing to do the heavy lifting required to do such things as build opt-in lists. If you don't have enough 'hard work' packed, you will be tempted to believe that you can make money without having to work. You must expect to work very hard. Check!

› **Patience:** The Internet is supposed to have speeded everything up...and it did speed up a lot of things. Success, however, is not one of them. You will be required to use a lot of patience as you pursue success in the Internet jungle. Check!

› **Luck**: You will need a lot of 'luck', as well. However, you have to make your own luck as you travel through the Internet jungle. To make 'luck' you must have all of the other supplies in ample quantity. When you mix **ambition, determination, work ethic, time, hard work and patience** together in equal portions, you get what some people call **'luck'**. Check!

Conclusion

You have a lot of nerve! That is a compliment. It takes a lot of nerve to venture into any unknown situation but venturing into the jungle of Internet business takes a larger supply than usual.

Because you are not a person to ever be really satisfied with the Status Quo is why you have decided to look for an online work-at-home job or to start your own at-home business.

Not being satisfied with the Status Quo is an admirable quality and one that you should nurture and help to grow and thrive. Those who are unwilling to accept the way that things are now are the ones who change them and make better futures for themselves, their families and sometimes for the rest of the world.

In order to affect a change for a better future, you must have a clear plan for making those necessary changes. Remember that, 'Those who fail to plan, plan to fail'. You must have a clear destination and a detailed plan for the route that will get you to that destination.

"I want to work at home....or I want my own online business" is NOT a plan. That's a wish. Wishes do come true but rarely without a plan of action and a lot of hard work.

You must prepare yourself for a long and hard journey through the Internet jungle and you must be prepared for the lions, tigers, bears and sneaky snakes, as well as, for the cannibals and the unfriendly natives.

You must go well equipped and well supplied to face and defeat all of the dangers and obstacles that stand between you and your destination.

It is true that the Internet jungle is a dangerous place and one that is fraught with traps and obstacles that, at first glance, seem insurmountable.

It is also true that the Internet jungle is ripe with opportunity for those who have the ambition, drive and determination to venture into it and conquer it.

If you enjoyed this book, please consider reading my other published works.

The Book on Evil, Wicked, Mean, & Nasty

The Fine Art of Getting Even

The Ancient Wisdom of an Old Shadow Warrior

The Plucking of the Golden Years Goose

Rolling in Tradition:
The Story of Cigars and Tobacco

Ebook Entrepreneur:
Crafting Your Path To Profits

The Writer's Odyssey:
Crafting Your Literary Legacy, A New Writer's Guide Book

From Words to Wealth:
Mastering Freelance Writing

The Morning Elixir of Life:
The History and Art of Coffee

Ignite Your Motivation:
Achieve Your Dreams,

The Spice Cabinet Apothecary:
Natural Health at Your Fingertips

The Elderly Trap: Uncovering Scams and Reclaiming Security in the Golden Years.

The Author's Manual:
Navigating the How-To Writing Process,
Meditation Guide for Beginners
The Art of Personal Mastery:
A Roadmap to Success and Fulfillment

Did you love *How to Guidebook to the Internet Jungle Avoiding the scams and Traps*? Then you should read *EBook Entrepreneur: Crafting Your Path to Profit*[1] by Richard Krause!

2

Unleash Your Inner Wordsmith and Build a Thriving E-Book Empire!

Are you a passionate writer with dreams of sharing your knowledge, stories, or expertise with the world? Do you long for the freedom to work from the comfort of your own home while turning your words into a source of income? Look no further! ***"EBook Entrepreneur: Crafting Your Path To***

---

1. https://books2read.com/u/m2EyJ6

2. https://books2read.com/u/m2EyJ6

Profits" is your ultimate guide to stepping into the exciting world of e-book entrepreneurship.

In this comprehensive book, you'll discover: The Art of E-Book Creation: Unlock the secrets to crafting compelling e-Books that captivate readers from start to finish. Learn how to structure your content, engage your audience, and create e-books that stand out in a crowded digital market. Understanding Your Audience: Master the art of identifying and connecting with your target readers. Explore strategies to tailor your eBooks to their needs, ensuring your work resonates deeply with your audience. Effective Marketing Techniques: Launch your e-books into the digital stratosphere with proven marketing strategies. From building a strong online presence to leveraging social media, you'll learn how to promote your work and attract a loyal readership. Monetize Your Passion: Turn your love for writing into a profitable venture. Discover multiple revenue streams, including self-publishing, affiliate marketing, and more, to build a sustainable income from your e-Books. Success Stories: Be inspired by real-life E-Book Entrepreneurs who have turned their literary dreams into reality. Learn from their experiences and gain insights into the e-book industry's ever-evolving landscape.

Whether you're a seasoned author or a first-time writer, ***"EBook Entrepreneur: Crafting Your Path To Profits"*** equips you with the knowledge, strategies, and inspiration to embark on a journey of literary entrepreneurship. Join the ranks of successful EBook Entrepreneurs who have transformed their passion for writing into a thriving business.

If you're ready to embrace your inner wordsmith, chart your course to profits, and share your unique voice with the world, this eBook is your compass. Start your e-book entrepreneurship journey today, and watch your dreams take flight!

Read more at https://rkrause45.wixsite.com/mysite.

www.ingramcontent.com/pod-product-compliance
Lightning Source LLC
LaVergne TN
LVHW090414210926
848480LV00002B/566